Creating the World

Poetry, Art, and Children

Creating the World

Poetry, Art, and Children

John Carpenter

University of Washington Press   Seattle & London

This book was published with the assistance of a grant from the Andrew W. Mellon Foundation.

Copyright © 1986 by the University of Washington Press
Composition by University of Washington Department of Printing, Seattle
Printing and binding by Toppan Printing Company, Tokyo
Designed by Audrey Meyer

Library of Congress Cataloging-in-Publication Data

Carpenter, John.
  Creating the world.

  Bibliography: p.
  1. Children's writings, American. 2. Visual poetry, American.
3. Prose poetry, American. 4. School prose, American.
5. Creative writing—Study and teaching. 6. Children's art—United States.
I. Title
PS508.C5C37   1986   811'.54'0809282   85-40354
ISBN 0-295-96261-5 (cloth)
ISBN 0-295-96384-0 (pbk.)

Cloth edition: Lettering for binding design created by Marc Bianchi, 3rd grade,
Osborn School, Rye, New York

Printed and bound in Japan
10 9 8 7 6 5 4 3 2 1

Contents

penicillim in
looks the
like stars
a planet
hiding

Richard Pack
3d grade
Viewlands Elementary

Preface

This study is intended for readers interested in the visual and language arts in the broadest sense and in the creative process itself. I hope it will speak to all those who have a concern for the arts and the psychology of the arts, whether as parents or teachers or practitioners and students of the contemporary arts today.

The poems presented here are by children from kindergarten through the twelfth grade. During the years 1974 to 1982 I was poet-in-residence and writing specialist for the Seattle Public Schools, and it was then that I first formulated the ideas in this book. In the setting of a large, diversified city I was dealing with many different ages concurrently, and I was able to observe how each one had its own surprising aptitudes and special strengths. I developed a variety of activities and techniques to accompany the act of writing, and as the students and I worked together I made a number of discoveries. Writers like Kenneth Koch, and psychologists, such as Erik Erikson, D. W. Winnicott and Jean Piaget, have spoken of the relationship between learning and testing, or play. But I was struck, above all, by the very close relationship between the creative act and the act of learning. From the earliest age the existence of an observable surrounding reality—or cluster of realities—exerts an enormous attraction. Time after time I was able to witness the great power of the creative, or integrative, act: how it reaches beyond the paper, beyond the desk, beyond the classroom window, beyond the street, into the city in the distance or the past. This sense of an outer reality, stretching also inside the mind, was powerfully attractive, and was reinforced by the fine works by adults that I sometimes used as examples in class. Always—and always in varying combinations—the whole outside world would be available and present, poised at the threshold of the mind, in an act of attention: ready to be possessed and understood by the child, as by the adult, awaiting only the means, the tools of writing.

Some of the poems included here appeared in the anthologies *Chimneys, the Wind, and the Three Giants* (Seattle Public Schools, 1978), *Stealing the Moon and Stars* (Seattle Public Schools, 1978), and *The Creation of the World* (Seattle Public Schools, 1979). Some material was published in articles in *The Arts*, "Children and Words" (November 1979) and "Poetry in the Schools" (February 1979). Other poems appeared in the Arts section of the *Seattle Times* (January 1978), and some were silkscreened onto panels that appeared in the Seattle Metro buses. Because color is an important element of concrete or picture poems, a large number of the poems in the book were originally done in color.

I would like to express thanks to the English Office of the Seattle Public Schools, to Bob Mahan and Louise Markert; and to the Arts Office, to Judith Meltzer and Ray Thompson.

John Carpenter

Suma Love
grade 2

The world was just created and was also empty. Raven had felt very lonely in it. But one day when Raven was walking on the beach he saw a clam, and then a face peeked out, and then came out and then hid again. And then a whole bunch of faces came out and Raven said, "It's not lonely any more."

The End

1 / Introduction

Poetry and Space

This book is a study of the relation between the visual imagination and the verbal imagination. It is an exploration of the many different ways in which the two may be combined by people of different ages, and of the artistic use of space. Picture poems, or concrete poems, made by children from kindergarten through twelfth grade are the focus of the book, but it is also a study of different types of visual poems by adults.

The term "concrete poem" is increasingly used in the arts—"concrete" in the sense of "not abstract"—and refers to form that can be grasped by the senses, especially the eyes. A "concrete poem" includes both words and pictures. It is a poem that integrates verbal and visual elements in an artistic manner. There is not just a picture followed by words or words followed by a picture; rather, the verbal and visual elements reinforce one another throughout the composition. Usually the words themselves take on a visual shape. They are not visually neutral, and therefore they cannot be changed from cursive or printed to typed form without seriously altering the composition. The words may be arranged vertically or in a curved line, or the letters may be drawn to form a visual and not purely verbal pattern. Often color is used. The variety and number of ways in which words can be altered and combined with visual images is almost infinite. The purpose of using words and pictures together is expressive; the techniques are always elaborated gradually, through use, and are at the service of the meaning of the poem.

Students between ten and thirteen years of age—fourth grade through seventh grade—excel at this kind of poem. Why don't children who are younger than ten, or older than thirteen, succeed with quite the ease of the children within this age range? One reason, I believe, is that students learn cursive handwriting in the third grade. This liberates them from too close and too literal a dependence on the printed word. They learn that it is acceptable for words to slant, and that some personal freedom—how much always depends on the individual classroom teacher—is admissible in their own handwriting. Also they have made enough progress in spelling and writing that by the fourth grade the purely mechanical problems are no longer as important as they were in second and third grades. The mechanical instrument is now available, verbal self-expression becomes more of a realistic possibility. This is not to say that students in the primary grades cannot create good picture poems—they can. The genre is a very helpful device in teaching them verbal skills, and it often provides a marvelous incentive for learning to write. Picture poems written by the very young are presented and discussed in the first part of this book.

Children aged ten through thirteen often have an image in their minds which is simultaneously visual and verbal: it has shape, and often color, yet is associated with a word or words. If permitted, the students in this age range might spontaneously begin with a small picture and then shift to words, or they might start with a word or phrase and then shift to a visual image. Students between nine and thirteen tend to be natural, spontaneous drawers, but this ability often disappears in junior high school. There are a number of reasons for this: many students either stop drawing as frequently as they did when they were younger, or they might become interested in art courses and purely visual expression. In either case the *simultaneous* expression of verbal and visual elements is lost.

Eighth and ninth graders do not draw and paint less well than fifth graders, far from it—their drawings are often impressive in detail and basic construction; frequently there is perspective (first taught in the sixth-grade curriculum), shading, and convincing three-dimensional space. Yet no matter how accomplished the students may be, a show of hands of how many enjoy drawing will reveal a much smaller proportion than in the lower grades. The combination of the verbal and the visual will be less spontaneous. Usually one will be done first and then the other, each with its own momentum. And most important, color will no longer be used.

I believe the poems included in this book are very good, a few exceptionally so. I want to avoid extravagant claims because these poems are written by children who are neither great poets nor great artists; their verbal and artistic skills have yet to be fully developed. On the other hand, the integration of these skills is at an extremely high level. It is sufficient to compare these concrete or picture poems by students with those written by adults to realize that the poems written by students can be superior in some respects, especially in integration, the use of color, and expressiveness. The reader who looks through anthologies of concrete poetry by adults is bound to notice that a high proportion of the poems are dependent on machine graphics or technical gimmicks, and many are lacking in expressive content. Only a few of the better-known contemporary poets—for example, May Swenson and John Hollander—have experimented with the genre. The children's poems in this book do not depend on gimmicks of any kind; the poems are often highly expressive, containing considerable artistic originality and energy. Above all they excel in the integration of verbal and visual elements, the one reinforcing the other.

Contemporary concrete poetry written by adults gives the impression of being a young genre; some critics question its legitimacy altogether. I would like to state at the outset that I believe some is very good and some is very bad. Evaluative standards must be imposed on the genre, and its extreme apologists frequently fail to do this, thus giving the genre as a whole a bad name, which is unnecessary. Its origins are quite legitimate—it has grown out of poetry's traditional use of graphic space on the page. Indentations, different stanzaic shapes, and varying margins at both the beginning and the end of the poetic line are normal to poetry, just as the counting of syllables or accents is normal; the use of graphic form has an ancient lineage. Contrasting line lengths is another device used by great poets, among them Shakespeare:

There are more things in heaven and earth, Horatio,
Than are dreamt of in your philosophy.
But come;
Here, as before, never, so help you mercy . . .

        (*Hamlet*, I, v)

Twentieth-century poets such as Ted Hughes frequently use contrasting line lengths for expressive effect:

The wolf goes to and fro, trailing its haunches and whimpering horribly.
It must feed its fur.
The night snows stars and the earth creaks.

        (from *The Howling of Wolves*)

Concrete poetry has naturally grown out of this expressive use of the graphic space on the page. On the other hand, twentieth-century artists and painters (for example, Joan Miró) often use words, phrases, and sentences in their paintings. From the time of Cubism, when Picasso and Braque first introduced words into their canvases around 1910, until the present, twentieth-century painting has consistently sought to broaden its frontiers and include the expression of the written word. At its best, concrete poetry has tried to do something analogous by bringing graphic expression within the limits of the poem.

Poetry and Children

Most of the poems by children in this book were written in the classroom, at home, or in library conference rooms. Usually the students also wrote other types of poems with me: unrhymed or rhymed, collaborative poems, story poems, poems based on myths, word murals, lyrics, or poems using traditional forms, depending on the age and interest of the students. The concrete or visual poems in this book were never written as examples of a specialized branch of poetry. I would like to say a few words about the spirit in which we worked: always we wrote about experience, or ordinary everyday reality. The poems were not written as exercises nor for the purpose of display. On the contrary, we wrote about the most rudimentary, fundamental reality that surrounds us all.

We did not begin with the notion of writing poems or concrete poems but usually began with something that was visible. Perhaps we could see it from the classroom window—fog or rain, mountains if we were lucky, ferries, freeways, or a shopping center, roofs, chimneys, or other windows. Sometimes I brought objects into the classroom: walnuts or grapes, tools, a chess set, a television set removed from its surrounding plastic case, an old amplifier, pre-amplifier, and power supply. Or we discussed and drew objects which had suggestive shapes and appealed to the senses, like ginger root, eggplant, broccoli, garlic, artichokes, or moss. This visual contact with objects had the advantage of permitting us to look at them closely, intently. Usually they were very ordinary and familiar, of the kind that we all see every day but rarely notice.

It quickly became apparent that we knew very little about these objects. We did not know what their exact colors were or how to describe their shapes—it was as if there were large gray areas in our experience, in our memory, where the things with which we were the most familiar were lost or obscured. I am speaking not only of children but of myself and other adults as well. There are numerous causes for this: television, movies, and other passive forms of entertainment certainly play a large role, and so do our general attitudes about what is important and what not important, many of them subconscious. In 1962 a teacher and writer addressed a very similar question:

Are not children too often deprived of experience at first hand—or if not that, then are they not exposed to experiences following so closely, one upon the heels of the other, that there is no time to absorb, to assess, to do more than skim the surface of any single one?

(Flora Arnstein, *Poetry in the Elementary Classroom*)

What was the most striking was that often we had the greatest difficulty in describing the things with which we were most intimate. Here the fact that we could look at them carefully, sketch them, and ask questions about them from a variety of perspectives was a great benefit. The initial sketches helped us to familiarize ourselves with their visual nature, with shapes, forms, colors, parts. In all of these exercises reality came first and only later the poem followed. After we became familiar with the objects, the choice of words naturally arose, and we asked what is the best way to describe the sound of falling rain, the color of eggplant in shadow or light, or the movement of cars on a freeway. We looked for the best way to describe these—what really accounts for our experience and for what we can observe. To find the right word is not easy, either for children or for adults. In French this is called the search for the *mot juste*; with children it is a matter of the most basic verbal skill, and could be described in many ways—poetry or "language arts," "English," creative writing, possibly prose.

What was at stake was the basic relation between the individual and reality, whether he or she would express this relationship visually and verbally. I tried to foster a general aptitude for dealing with this reality, the essential object-to-eye-to-hand and mind coordination which is central to language arts and the basic school curriculum. I became increasingly convinced of the value of this approach when I observed that many students who were not necessarily the best spellers in the class or who had not previously done very well in tests excelled at this kind of poem. Often focusing too closely on words "frightens away" the experiences, and words seem remote and impersonal. The students might be special education students who are intimidated by the written word, and yet they might have superior originality, wit, and even ability to make puns and play with words if given the chance to express themselves orally. I found this especially true of minority students I worked with who frequently have great verbal gifts—for example, spontaneous alliteration—which they are not able to express with pencil and paper. If they are exposed to poetry as a specialized activity, they may find it irrelevant or useless, they may dislike it or not understand it. Instead, in my classes we would always focus on concrete reality or experience and *then* use words to express it. The words followed: they were subordinate, they were tools. As a result they were much more interesting and had greater weight.

Frequently the visual aspect of concrete reality would immediately excite students' interest. A great value of the concrete poem was that the verbal and the visual were not separated into different compartments but were united, as they are in the world of actual experience and everyday life. In the best concrete poems the verbal and visual elements constantly reinforce one another throughout the composition. Here, then, was a "poetry" which was not a specialized activity opposed to a broader and more universal reality— clearly, it would always lose in any attempt to compete with reality if defined in these terms. Instead, it was a poetry that was at the center of the individual's relationship to reality.

The poems in the first three sections of this book were written by children from kindergarten through twelfth grade, and the final section is a discussion of concrete poems by adult poets and painters. It is a large age range. The child's perspective of reality constantly changes, and this is fully reflected in the poems—with each year new skills are acquired, sometimes old skills are lost. One of the most interesting aspects of these poems is that they mirror the development of the child so faithfully, and that the child's relation to the world and to space can be seen in them so clearly. Chapter 2 contains poems by children in kindergarten through third grade. These children have begun to relate words to the world around them, and although their oral verbal ability is considerable, they do not possess the mechanics of writing. Chapter 3 contains poems written by children from the fourth through the seventh grades. Chapter 4 deals with poems written by students in the seventh and eighth grades and high school, when the student's relationship to the concrete world and space undergoes many changes. The fifth chapter is a study of the relation of visual and verbal elements in adult art.

2 / Kindergarten to Third Grade

Children in kindergarten do not yet know how to write; sometimes they are taught the letters of the alphabet, but writing usually starts in the first grade. Yet they can speak well; they can also make vivid, expressive drawings and paintings. When their words are transcribed by another, they create very interesting poems, especially class poems or class collaborations. The whole class may write this kind of poem together: the poet or teacher asks the class a series of questions about a theme or event, students who have ideas raise their hands, they are called on to say their ideas aloud, the teacher then writes the ideas on the blackboard, treating each as a fragment of a poem or perhaps a whole line. As the questions progress, the blackboard is slowly filled up. When the class is over, the teacher transcribes all the material onto a piece of paper, then later rearranges the lines, modifies the poem or shortens it, using only the students' words. At the next class meeting the teacher reads the poem aloud to the students, and almost always they are pleased with the outcome.

It is possible for a teacher or poet to write down a poem which an individual student in kindergarten says orally; however, this requires the presence of other teachers to take care of the rest of the class, and it is not a very practical activity. Once, as an experiment, I used fifth graders as scribes for children in a kindergarten I was visiting. First the kindergarteners made two watercolor paintings apiece, of the rain and outer space—that is, the way they imagined outer space. Then we wrote class poems on each of these subjects. I asked them a variety of questions, and the teacher transcribed their answers onto a large piece of butcher paper tacked over the blackboard.

The next day we took the entire kindergarten class upstairs to the fifth-grade classroom. The kindergarteners took their stools with them as well as the two watercolor paintings they had made; inside the fifth-grade room they paired off with the fifth graders, each kindergartener sitting next to a fifth grader. The butcher paper with the class poem written on it the day before was attached to the blackboard at the front of the room, and I read their ideas aloud to refresh their memories. Then each fifth grader was permitted to write down on one of the watercolor paintings whatever words the kindergartener next to him wanted written—ideas or phrases from the class poem on the butcher paper, or totally new ideas which occurred on the spur of the moment. The fifth graders, who had written poems with me before, were not permitted to use their own words, only those of the kindergarteners next to them. They were scribes, or robot arms. Usually they asked the kindergarteners what the shapes represented, to become familiar with the painting before beginning to write. Each fifth grader could put the words where he or she wanted and combine them with the shapes of the painting in a meaningful way.

Although it might seem that I took great pains to obtain poems from children who are not capable of writing, the results were extremely interesting. Kindergarteners, and to a certain extent first graders, are at a stage of development very different from that of children between six and twelve years of age. They are closely attached to their parents and for the most part do not conceive of a world beyond the family circle. The child of four or five does not clearly distinguish between make-believe and reality, although soon this stage will end. It is quite natural that writing should begin in the first grade because it is at that time the child becomes more interested in the outside world and the tools which are used there. In kindergarten, however, children write a special kind of poem, full of expression, spontaneity, feeling, and, often, fears. Their poems are imaginative but the imagination is completely fused with reality, as is illustrated by this class poem about lying in bed:

IN BED

When I've been put in bed
I can see my fish, silver and gold,
the dark part of my next-door neighbor's house
and dark trees in the garden.
Just before sleep the last things I see
are cars, trucks, my pillow—
my rug looks like a monster, always curled up,
it seems it has eyes. It bounces.
I see little brown creatures under my bed
and my attic scares me, there are things hanging down,
they are little balls
and my cat plays with them.
When I take my beaver to bed with me
I see the big shadow of the beaver
and I get scared!
My hallway scares me,
there is a record of Dracula with creepies
on it and it crawls on me.
The last things I hear are dogs barking outside,
my sister crying
and a guitar,
it sounds like a mouse crossing the strings
then I start to dream:
it is like falling off a cliff,
Godzilla is shooting me with her lasers,
the wind says Oooooooooo I come to get a little kid.
It feels like swallowing a hundred caterpillars.

—*Laurelhurst Elementary, Mrs. Kurose's kindergarten class*

When I read aloud the class poem by kindergarteners about outer space—about the various monsters they imagined there who were "alive," "slimey," "icky," and "gooey"—the kindergarteners became excited all over again, many of them saying "Oooh" and "Ahh," while the fifth graders next to them were completely unmoved, unable to understand the excitement. In a year or two the children in kindergarten would soon join the fifth graders by crossing the boundary into a different stage of development. In the meantime, fantasy and reality remained largely identical for the kindergarteners, and their vivid, seemingly abstract drawings—not abstract to them—were full of color. On the oral level their verbal ability was considerable; one student started his poem on rain: "A rainbow looks like a colorful racetrack in the sky."

In psychological terms, this attitude toward the outside world has been described as "spatial egocentrism": the child still does not describe the world or space using an objective reference system. Subjective space and objective space merge, and the task of sorting them out is accomplished only gradually. Very young children slowly build and coordinate their ideas about space as they develop other notions about the world. That is, they learn from actual manipulation of objects, not merely by passive observation. In infancy space is probably no more than concrete "spaces" surrounding given objects. Slowly, in the course of development, the many "spaces" are constructed into an abstract idea: one space. This process has been described by Piaget as "decentration" or the decentering of the child's attention from his egocentric point of view.

In the poem beginning with the words "Outer space is scarey . . ." the objective world and subjective world are very closely united.

Rain was a topic that proved to be very suggestive, both visually and verbally, to kindergarteners and to all elementary-school students. Three poems by kindergarteners are about rain: "Rain goes straight," "The rain makes a big noise," and "Rain is curved. . . ." The pictures were painted when rain was falling outside the window and we could observe it. When the paintings were finished, we followed the same procedure as with the poems on outer space: we discussed the rain, how it falls, what sounds it makes, what it reminds us of, and then we wrote a class poem. The following day the class joined the fifth graders, who acted as scribes, integrating the words of the kindergarteners with the shapes of their paintings.

In the first grade, students begin to write words—large words. Here as with the kindergarten students it is possible to pursue oral techniques, to write class poems or experiment with dictation, but poetry is probably most useful in helping the students themselves to write. There is a big difference between their abilities at the beginning of the year and at the end; in the autumn they know no more than the kindergarteners, but soon they can copy, and if the words are their own, the results are original. The poems must be short. It is beneficial once again to use the class poem and also to make colored pictures. The class poem using the children's own words can be fairly long when it is read aloud to the class—they usually like long poems when the words are their own—but when it is written on the blackboard the next day, about six of the best lines should be selected and copied by the teacher in large, clear printing. At the beginning of the year probably even fewer lines

Dionna Smith

Outer space is scarey
there would be space creatures
there would be lots of wrecked up space ships

dionna

You
would
be able
to see
lots of
planets
there would
be lots of
stars
there would
be lots of
flowers

it would be really cold
it would be really dark
you would keep going
          down and down
there would be slimey
                    monsters
martian dogs
giant martian birds
    martian cats
    lots of smoke
    martian robots.

Portia Beard,
            scribe

17

Rain goes straight

Rain goes crooked

It goes in clear glass

It sounds like click Click Click

It's old as a drug store

The rain is brown and white

The rain is red and blue

Purple and pink

It drops on my

head and glass

Trina
Hedin

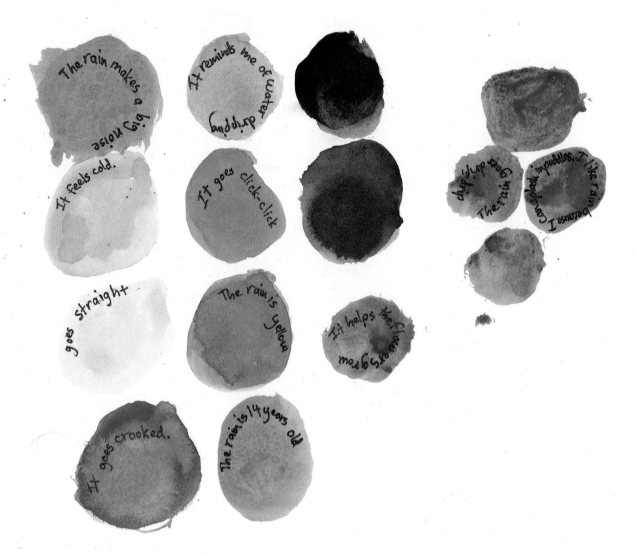

The rain makes a big noise

It feels cold.

goes straight

It goes crooked.

It reminds me of water dripping.

It goes click-click

The rain is yellow

The rain is 14 years old

The rain goes drip-drip

The rain goes drip-drip. I can splash in puddles. I like rain because I

It helps the flowers grow.

Erin Okawa

19

Somebody put a little seed and grows into a cloud. and grows and grows into the sky and it grows

Rain is curved because the wind blows it to the left.

Sometimes the little drops go straight.

Then the rain stops.

A rain bow looks like half of a circle.

the rainbow is purple, orange, blue and green

Chris Green

should be used: if the blackboard is too full the students will not be able to recognize their own words. The students can then copy onto their pictures whatever lines they like best, and if they have new ideas they are free to use them, asking the teacher for help with the spelling. The advantage of having the lines from the class poem on the blackboard is that the words are clearly written and correctly spelled. Copying them is a useful exercise in itself, and the words have special meaning for the students when combined with their own pictures.

The two poems beginning with the lines "It's a rainy color" and "It's soft," were written about fog. During the previous week there had been thick fog every morning, occasionally lifting around lunchtime. We wrote a class poem about the fog and I made two versions, one longer and this short version of eight lines. All the words came from the students in the class.

FOG

It's a rainy color,
you could put it inside your coat.
It's soft, once I was playing with my friend
and my friend disappeared.
The fog was softer than a door.
If I were the fog I would touch flowers, grass,
I would touch a barn,
it would be smooth.

The picture poem "It's a rainy color" uses the first and fifth lines. "It's soft" uses the third and fourth lines.

Many poems by first graders just beginning to write contain messages to their parents, usually their mothers. In the poem, "The sun sets . . . ," the student has accepted the invitation to put new ideas in the poem, reminding us that the first grade is not just the beginning of one stage but it is also the end of another, and that the transition requires some time. If a first grader writes "Mom I love you" in the middle of his poem, he is testifying to the spontaneity of his creative act, a pencil between his own hands and the ability to form his own message bridging the distance from school to home. This is still what is often called the oedipal period, roughly the ages between three and six or seven, when a wide variety of psychological events coincide to reinforce each other and propel the infant into childhood.

It's a rainy color fog

CloVER
Benton grade 1

The fog was softer than a door.

It's soft. Once I was playing with my friend and my friend disappeared.

Karama

Hawkins, grade 1, McGilvra Elementary

The Sunsets
Mom + Mom
sitting on a
rocket
pumpkin

Jerry Williams
Grade 1
McGilvra Elementary

24

It is during the period from six to twelve years of age that each individual learns to get along in a more complicated, or "grown-up," manner. The learning process at this stage does not require much additional physical development. The rate of physical growth abruptly slows between six and ten years old to almost half the previous rate; it will not speed up again until early adolescence. During the new stage children become ready to apply themselves to given skills and tasks. Because of their increasing abilities they have more contact with people outside the family and with wider aspects of the world. They go to school. They learn the use of tools, how to conduct themselves outside of the family, and to think for themselves.[1]

During this new stage the child becomes ready to apply himself to given skills and tasks. Because of his increasing abilities he can have more contact with people outside the family and with wider aspects of the world. He goes to school. He adjusts himself to the laws of tools, he learns to conduct himself in the world outside the family and to think for himself.

In the sequence of poems about clouds, "This one is a nimbus," "It's like a hand . . . ," and "Away to cloud land," the students are primarily reacting to the shapes and forms of clouds that they are actually watching—they are using their senses, especially sight. Although some of the metaphors are subjective, many were suggested by close observation.

In the poem by Jason Omenn, "The sun giant is big," the "three giants" are the sun, the ocean, and the moon, when they all can be seen together during the daytime. This was a summer poem; we talked about the beach where we could see the "three giants," which were not, however, visible before the students' eyes as they made their poems.

1. Arnold Gesell, *Infancy and Human Growth* (New York: Macmillan, 1928), pp. 334–54. See also Charles Darwin, *The Expression of the Emotions in Man and Animals* (New York: Appleton and Co., 1897), pp. 369–90; and Benjamin Spock, *Baby and Child Care* (New York: Pocket Books, 1973), p. 389.

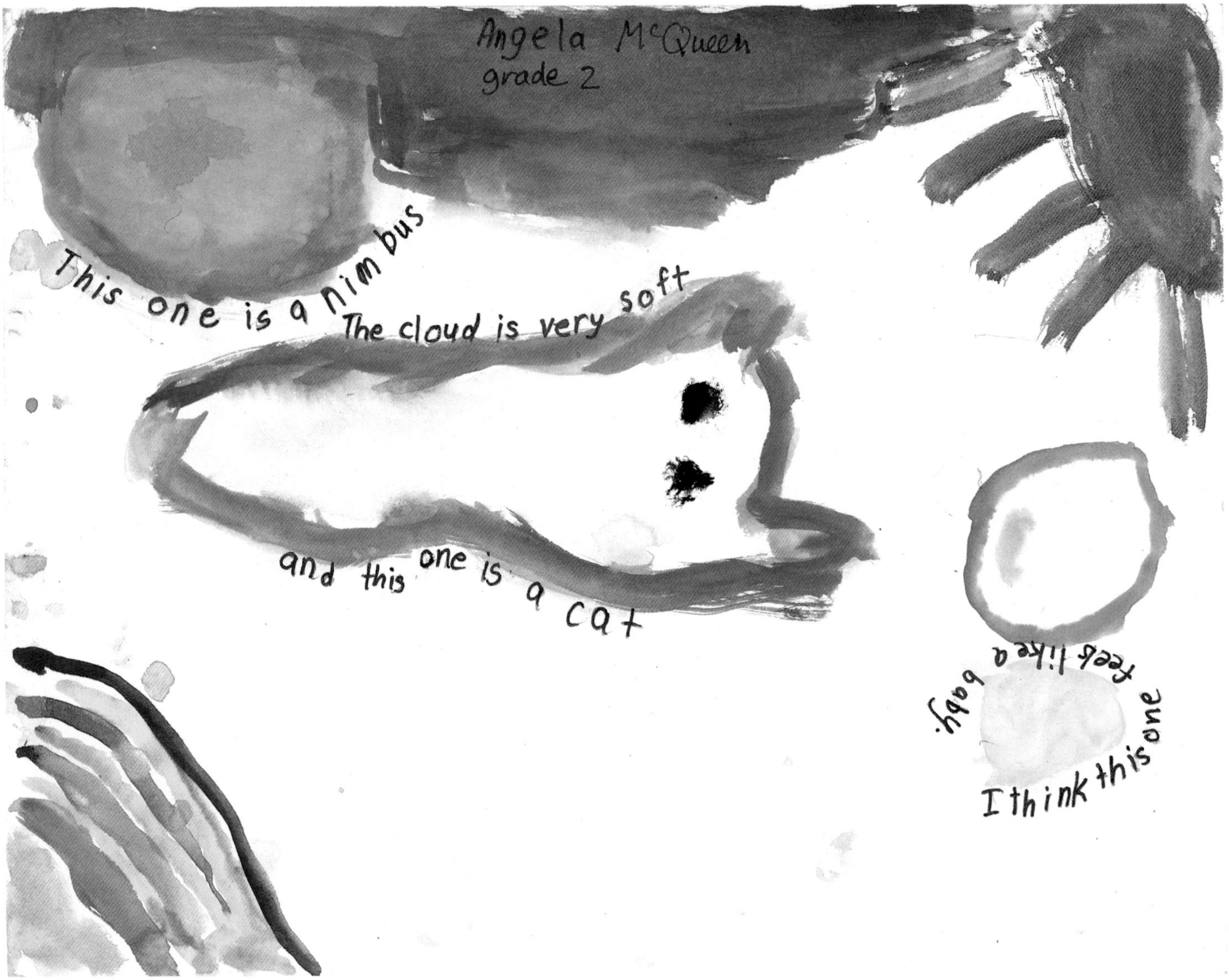

Angela McQueen
grade 2

This one is a nimbus
The cloud is very soft

and this one is a cat

I think this one
feels like a baby.

26

It looks like a blob from outer space.

It's like a hand reaching down to pick up a cloud

It looks like Godzilla of the water coming out

Jerod Gillies
2nd grade

27

clouds
are fluffy

Clouds
are
nice

Clouds
are very
swift.

thunder

Hello

This is the
land of cloud
I feel funny
when I go here.

Clouds
are
all
above
me.

a way to cloud land

The way
to
cloud
land

Michael
Crumpler
3-11-82

Here I am at the bottom.

it glows like a ball. The moon looks like

The sun giant is big.

The ocean looks smooth at night.

The beach is peach colored.

Jason Omenn
1 grade

Laura Sherman
3d grade

One year a long time ago the fog picked a very very pretty meadow to lay and rest on.

In spring every year a deep fog picks a meadow to lay and rest on.

This meadow had fish like birds and all things and flowers and weeds. And the fog lay down and enjoyd itself. While all the animals wondered what it is doing. So the fog told the animals about the itself. animals worrying peace. And every year this fog comes back. and let the fog lay in So stopped

Myths and Legends

Myths and legends are often evocative subjects for poems. Some of the non-Biblical creation myths are extremely concrete and appeal strongly to the visual imagination. A Northwest Indian myth about Raven and the creation of mankind from a clam[2] is straightforward and seemed to present no difficulties. The children were asked to retell the legend; what they wrote could be called a story poem, recounting one of the simplest legends about Raven. With the first graders I read the legend aloud, and while the class as a whole retold it orally, their version was written on the blackboard by their teacher. Then each student copied the class poem in part or in whole on paper. The second and third graders did not need to have the poem written on the blackboard, and after hearing the myth, wrote their own versions directly onto paper.

Some students would spontaneously alter and revise the myths in an imaginative manner, while others would stick closer to a literal interpretation. The need to select and integrate words with shapes ensured that both types of poems were personal, individual creations. In some poems, such as the one beginning "One year a long time ago . . . " (p. 30), the myth that provided a starting point for the poem is almost entirely lost to view.

In the second grade, students already know how to write many words; the distinction between themselves and the outside world becomes sharper, as does the difference between waking and sleeping. The poem beginning "I was walking on a leaf" (p. 32), is a remarkable example of a second grader's ability to remember a dream, and describe it in words and a picture. She is treating it as a dream, not as if it was the same as waking life, yet her recall is excellent. The next poem, also by a second-grade girl, is about migrating salmon; the student imagines that she is the salmon and compares the return of the salmon to a dream.

The curiosity of children leads them to observe objects around them—they are capable of describing these objects attentively and accurately, noticing a large range of characteristics or peculiarities. Poetry makes use of the same curiosity that is fundamental to science; the goal of each is to describe the world and reality. Third graders often use microscopes in the classroom, and it was only natural to bring language to bear on what they were observing. I once used a microprojector to cast microscopic images onto a screen and permit all of us to look at them together. The projector could magnify a specimen four hundred times. The images were extremely suggestive. The class was entranced by their shapes and by the discrepancy between the microscopic world and what they could observe with the naked eye. As images of different specimens were projected, the class members would express their interest, surprise, and even awe, in a manner analogous to that of the kindergarteners when they were imagining outer space. With the third graders, however, there was a greater sense of wonder and a real, strong sense of a vast outer world in which they were living. This world included themselves, which was brought home to them when they looked at cells taken from one of the students' mouths and projected onto the screen.

2. Marius Barbeau, *Haida Myths* (Ottawa: National Museum of Canada Bulletin 127, 1953).

I was walking on a leaf as it was flying through the air it was so scarey

Jill Chelimer

Jennifer

scary and
you feel like it's never going to stop.
I would like to jump into a cloud and sleep
a dark frightening feeling
like a fishy mystery
like going on for ever and ever
like having a bad dream

like falling down down down in a deep dark hole
I was a salmon swimming on and on.

In the third grade students learn cursive handwriting, and this seemed to help them combine words and lines of words with pictures. Perhaps the fact that words are permitted to slant gave students a sense of increased freedom with the written line, which gained greater continuity and flow. The words were more integrated with the shapes of the pictures, and less subordinate than with younger children. They often seemed to have greater authority than before.

The class also wrote a fine class collaboration about the images cast by the microprojector onto the screen:

MICROSCOPE

Cotton candy, firey red,
the cells could be a carnation
or the surface of the planet Mars—
they could be the Earth, the Moon and stars all together.
They could be the stained window in a church
or a firecracker, an "April Shower,"
a torch in a California Candle—
a spinning wheel changing colors.

If our room was magnified 400 times
it would be like twenty giants stacked together,
a fly would be twice as tall as a person.
If your money was 400 times bigger
you'd be a lot richer,
everyone in the school would come
and chip out pieces.
We wouldn't be able to sit at our desks—
I'd sneak under the door crack
or make a giant paper airplane
and fly for the door knob.
I'd cry for my Mom.
I'd be scared.

  —*Viewlands Elementary School, third grade*

The last poem in this section, "Fog is light, clouds are dark," is about fog. It is written by a fourth grader and has succeeded in integrating a visual picture and words very closely with one another.

Matt Carlson
3d grade

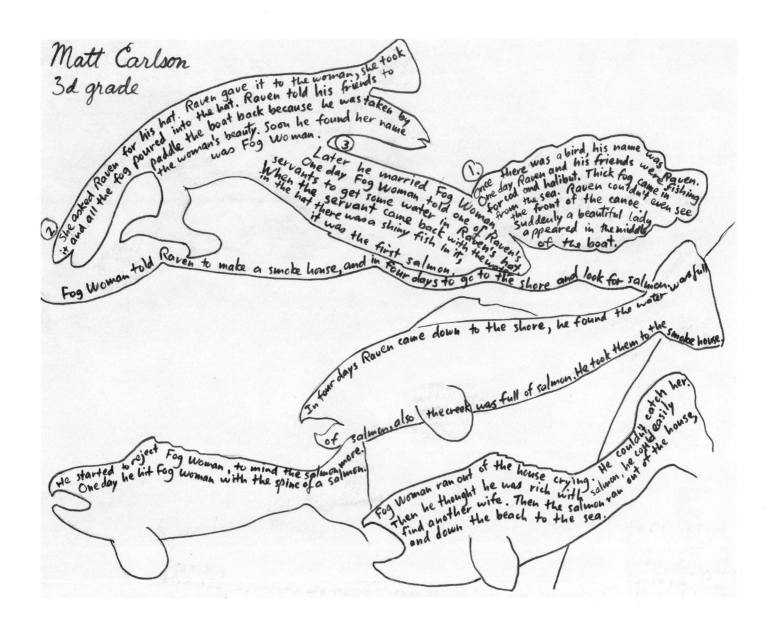

She asked Raven for his hat. Raven gave it to the woman, she took it and all the fog poured into the hat. Raven told his friends to paddle the boat back because he was taken by the woman's beauty. Soon he found her name was Fog Woman.

Once there was a bird, his name was Raven. One day Raven and his friends were fishing for cod and halibut. Thick fog came in from the sea. Raven couldn't even see the front of the canoe. Suddenly a beautiful lady appeared in the middle of the boat.

Later he married Fog Woman. One day Fog Woman told one of Raven's servants to get some water in Raven's hat. When the servant came back with the water in the hat there was a shiny fish in it, it was the first salmon.

Fog Woman told Raven to make a smoke house, and in four days to go to the shore and look for salmon.

In four days Raven came down to the shore, he found the water was full of salmon, also the creek was full of salmon. He took them to the smoke house.

He started to reject Fog Woman, to mind the salmon more. One day he hit Fog Woman with the spine of a salmon.

Fog Woman ran out of the house crying. He couldn't catch her. Then he thought he was rich with salmon, he could easily find another wife. Then the salmon ran out of the house, and down the beach to the sea.

35

Fog is light, clouds are dark, it's a peak of snow. It feels soft, I feel like jumping on it. It's a vanishing act, it feels like sand on me.

Janine
Parker
4th grade

A white floor, it is wet and squishy. It looks like a pillow.

I love fog, it's cold and wet, but it's ok. It's fun to see through. I look at fog a lot, sometimes I like to touch it.

36

3 / Fourth Grade to Seventh Grade

By the fourth grade children have mastered the mechanics of writing and spelling, and verbal expression is a real possibility. Between kindergarten and third grade the ability for visual expression was often ahead of verbal ability, but by the fourth grade the two are more or less equal. Visual aptitude continues to increase, especially drawing; students in the fourth- to seventh-grade range often prefer to use colored pencils, felt-tip pens, or crayons, and they become increasingly accurate. They have the same visual spontaneity of the younger students, and if the members of a class are asked how many of them like to draw almost all will raise their hands.

When making a picture poem they will often start with a preliminary sketch, but the words will usually follow upon the drawn lines very closely. The line may "break into" words, or, vice versa, the words may in turn call forth lines, drawn shapes, or colors. The simultaneity of verbal and visual expression is what is most striking about the poems in Chapter 3, done by children from nine to twelve years old. Their poems are fascinating and often surpass the concrete poems by adults, especially in the ability to combine visual and verbal elements.

This ability does not come at a new stage of development. Fourth and fifth graders are essentially in the same physical and psychological stage as second and third graders, although this is disguised by the great difference in acquired skills. The basic fact that second and third graders have not yet mastered the mechanics of writing hinders them from making individual poems, although their oral development is already considerable. Orally, second and third graders often express great wit, they can play with words, make puns, neologisms, homonyms. Third graders frequently write the most wildly imaginative class poems. But all of this must usually wait for the fourth grade before the written instrument is in hand, and students can write their own poems as individuals, without help.

The ability to express themselves simultaneously with words and pictures in the period from fourth to seventh grade deserves some comment. If visual aptitude was much greater than verbal, there would be no need to combine the two, and the child could continue making pictures on the one hand, and learn to write on the other, in order to acquire a necessary tool. When the verbal ability is much greater than the visual, pictures are often a distracting element that compromises the work and should best be omitted. This is sometimes the case in high school, and later in adulthood. But in the fourth- through seventh-grade range the verbal and visual operate together spontaneously and reinforce one another. Often if you try to omit the words, the picture is less expressive. It can be said that some picture poems are especially successful visually and others are successful verbally, but usually these elements combine throughout the composition, and this is particularly noticeable in the manner of composition. One element does not come first and the other second: they usually alternate, intermingling in all the major areas of the picture. It is the integration of these elements that stands out. The words reinforce the lines, the shapes, and the colors; in turn the colors, lines, and shapes pick up the meanings of the words, carrying them further into the space of composition. The mutual reinforcement constantly spreads, grows, and expresses. Perhaps this is one of the strongest arguments against the machine graphics and typography of adult concrete poems because the typed signs blend less easily with the hand-drawn visual elements. They stand out and in many respects represent a different medium of expression, made not by hand but by machine. Calligraphy and the hand-drawn word have much greater continuity with the visual shapes or lines of a picture and can integrate these, reinforce them, make them expressive more effectively.

I will leave it to the reader to judge these compositions. Clearly some are better and some are less good; they are all interesting. I do not think that everything children do is necessarily creative or artistic. Clearly there are many things adults can do better, but this is a type of poem at which children can excel. Many adult artists have not yet tried to develop this type of integrated or reinforced composition, concentrating instead on more specialized modes of expression. Perhaps in the future more artists and poets will turn to this new genre.

Rain

The procedure for writing poems about rain with fourth and fifth graders was similar to that for the poems written by kindergarteners, but with the older group the actual observation of rain falling outside the window was more important. The students wanted to stay longer at the window, sketching the rain and observing how it fell, whether or not at an angle. Could they see the individual drops, or were they more like lines, or columns? How does rain look in relation to the clouds above, to the roofs, streets, and trees? What does the rain sound like when individual drops first begin to hit? When the drops speed up and you no longer hear them individually, what does the rain sound like? Does it remind you of voices, or a musical instrument? A bassoon? What color is it? At the same time we would do a class poem, filling the blackboard with ideas and answers to these questions, but usually I did not bother to transcribe this material onto a piece of paper and arrange a class poem afterwards. I was more interested in the individual poems, and the board work was primarily intended to stimulate the imagination, to help students start their poems. They did not need to do any copying.

We would also discuss different possibilities of combining words with shapes. Often I showed them a copy of the poem by Guillaume Apollinaire, "Il pleut" (see p. 135), which is a superb example of a concrete poem, or "calligramme," as he called it. The students were not expected to understand French but simply to enjoy the graphic distribution of words on the page. Then the students would be given time to write their own poems. It was a four-step process: first, the quick sketch, then oral work collected on the blackboard, then discussion of the possibilities of combining words and shapes accompanied by some examples, and, finally, the writing of the individual poems. The last step—the most important—required more time at the fifth-grade level than with the younger students.

In the poem, "The rain comes down, down . . ." (p. 40), vertically arranged words interpenetrate the falling colored drops, freely mixing with them. The space for the words is the same as the space for the shapes; they blend harmoniously. Like the rain, the poem is "written" in the air between the clouds and the ground. The drops are stylized and have five different colors; they were drawn with felt-tip pens. The rain also has a light blue background made with a crayon. The colors express the sounds of the rain as well as its subjective evocations, emphasized by the author's action of closing her eyes "tight." Color, sound, and movement are very closely combined in this poem.

Elizabeth
Nelson

I like the sound of rain. I like the pitter patter sound, or it makes a tap tap sound. When the raindrops fall from the sky onto the ground, it makes a gives me a warm spring feeling instead of a cold feeling. I like it better when the rain is all different colors. Sometimes I close my eyes tight and imagine that the rain is different colors. The rain comes down down down and lands on the ground with a splash.

40

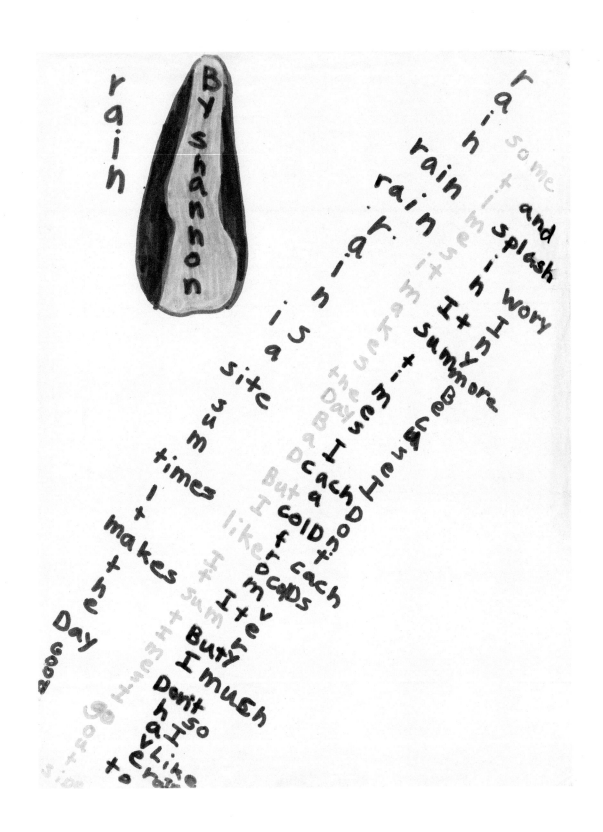

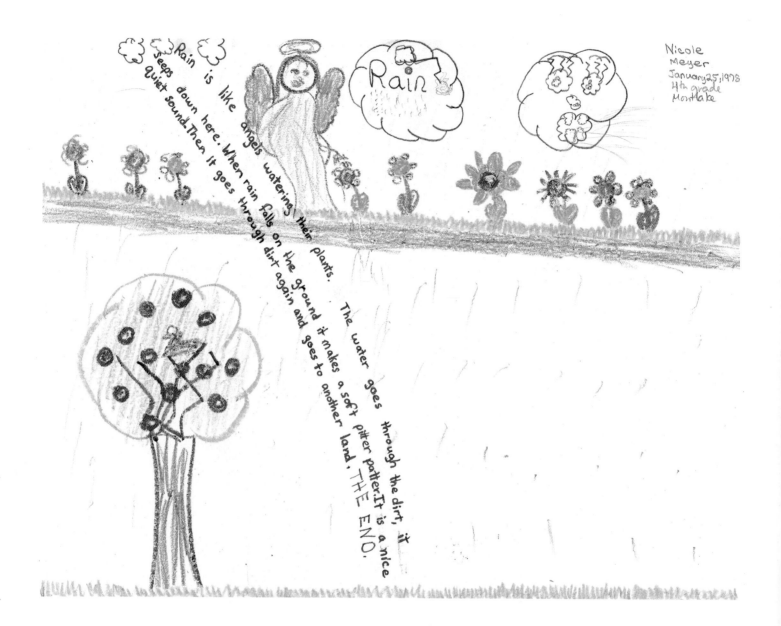

Rain is like angels watering their plants. When rain falls on the ground it makes a soft pitter patter. It is a nice quiet sound. Then it goes through dirt again and seeps down here. The water goes through the dirt, it goes to another land. THE END.

Rain

Nicole
Meyer
January 25, 1978
4th grade
Montlake

Nancy
Canady
4th grade
Montlake

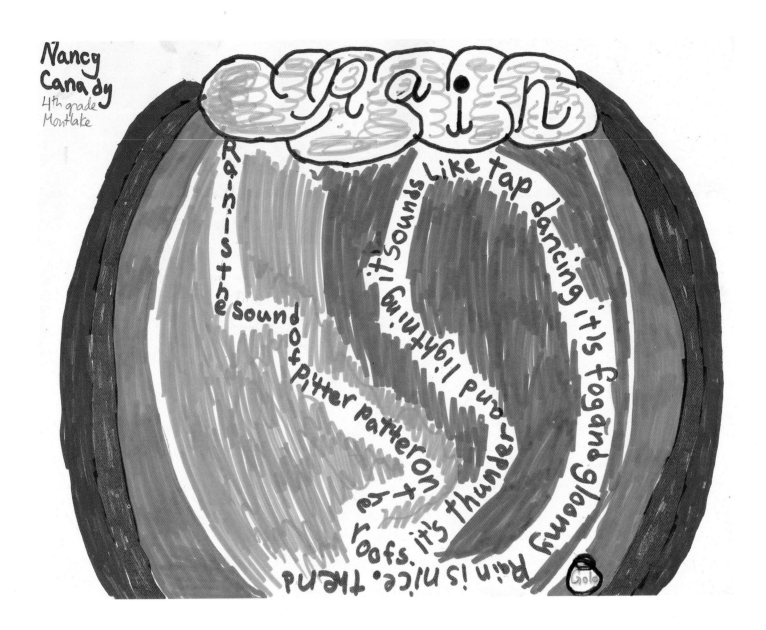

Rain is the sound of pitter patter on the roofs. It's thunder and lightning it sounds like tap dancing it's fog and gloomy Rain is nice. the end

43

Roofs

Roofs have a remarkable ability to excite the visual imagination. In discussing and sketching roofs we would notice their shapes, their colors, what they looked like when the sun hit them, and what different materials they were made of. In a sense it was an "artist's poem"—but it was always interesting to observe how a discussion of what seemed to be purely visual elements led to the need for words, and this can be seen in the poems. Also, the roofs were not seen exclusively in pictorial terms; in many poems the description of the roofs led to the notion of home, of the place where we live. Some of the poems about roofs were surprisingly stylized and abstract in their final form.

Karin Anderson's poem, "Roof," dispenses with the single straight line, and the roof is composed of words without an enclosing outline. Words form the roof as if they were horizontal shingles (just as words compose the chimney in the poem on page 52 like bricks). In the three main sections of the poem the words go in three different directions—horizontally, vertically, and in a circle. The central and largest section represents a roof observed at many different times, and it turns out to be many roofs telescoped into one.

The poem by Ben Hattrup (p. 48) uses many devices and is almost an anthology of the different ways in which words can be made to assume shapes. The weather vane on the roof between the television antenna and the chimney is a rooster made out of words, with a red comb sketched on the head. The words at the bottom describing the gutter end not with a period but with a drop. The words for color are colored, the words for shapes mimic the shapes they describe.

The next two poems, "I think a roof is shaped like a dome" and "Roofs have many different colors," are good examples of picture poems that are not literal or representational. Todd Staheli's poem is quite abstract and stylized, as are many concrete poems by adult painters and poets. The notion that roofs have an infinite variety of shapes is expressed by a series of different-colored irregular concentric circles. Susann Valiere's poem includes a recognizable girl, and although the words above her follow the appropriate inverted V of a roof, they also seem to be like thoughts and are not supported by any walls.

Karin Anderson
6th grade
John Rogers Elementary
School

DARK SMOKE LAZILY PUFFING OUT

ROOF. SHELTER. SLANTING SLOPE. RED. BLACK. DARK BROWN.
SPARKLING AS THE SUN HITS IT. CONTOURED. SQUIRREL
PATTERING. MYSTERIOUS FIGURE WALKING. PITTER PATTER MICE.
RAINDROPS PATTERING LIKE TINY FEET FLEEING ON THE ROOF.
CRACKLING. SNAPPING. NEVER QUIET. HAILSTONES AS NOISY AS
TINY PEBBLES BOUNCING. FALLING FROM A HIDDEN HAND. CONCRETE.
ASPHALT. TAR. SHINGLES. TILES. TAR PAPER. HOT ON MY BARE FEET.

LIKE A TINY WATERFALL CASCADING HURRIEDLY DOWNWARD.

Roofs make many different sounds, sometimes they sound like squirrels running around or rain drops dropping down. There are scary sounds too like the wind howling through the roof or the roof creaking and crackling and mice running around in the attic.

By Sherri Cheyne, 6th grade, John Rogers Elementary School

46

Dienstake Lucy Bundy

Roofs can be triangular. Roofs can be square. Roofs are blue, green, yellow, and gray. Colors of roofs are very gay. I wish I could

become a roof someday. Sometimes the moon and the stars are way up by mars. Stand on the roof. Then

Allicapoof! You are not a roof.

THEY HAVE TV AN-TENNAS

SOME HAVE EVEN WEATHER VANES AND

AND EVEN CHIMNEYS

ROOFS CAN BE MADE OF BRICK, TAR, SHINGLES, AND WOOD

THEY CAN BE BLUE, COLORED BLUE, RED, GREEN, TAN BROWN PURPLE SKY

THEY CAN BE SHAPED, SLANTED 8" BY 10 LEVEL, FLAT, TRIANGLE, SLANT, STEEP POINTED

THERE IS EVEN A MULTIPLE CHOICE OF GUTTERS AND THINGS LIKE THAT

BEN HATTRUP 4th grade, Montlake Elementary School

48

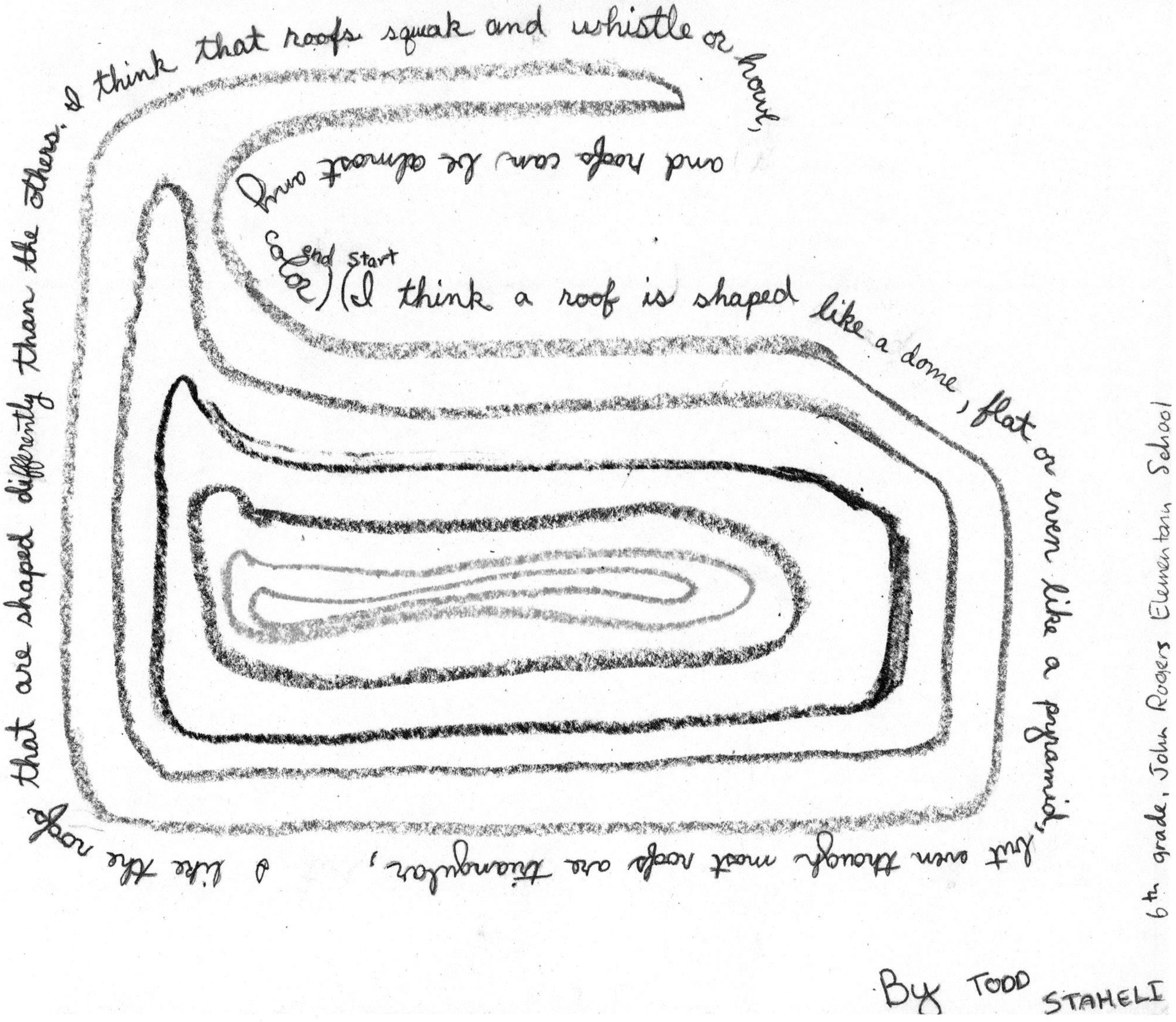

(I think a roof is shaped like a dome, flat or even like a pyramid, but even though most roofs are triangular, I like the roof that are shaped differently than the others. I think that roofs squeak and whistle or howl, and roof can be almost any color.)

start end

By TODD STAHELI

6th grade, John Rogers Elementary School

49

By Susann Valiere, 6th grade, John Rogers Elementary School

Chimneys

Often the view from a classroom window includes a variety of different chimneys, especially in the older sections of a city. Chimneys can be interesting and are typical of many ordinary, everyday objects that most people take for granted and rarely observe. In newly developed suburbs they are sometimes less suggestive, but frequently they reflect different architectural styles which give them the "personality" of the period; they can easily be compared with different kinds of people or parts of the body.

The author of the poem on page 55 is the daughter of a professional chimney sweep. The words start at the top of the chimney and descend, going down the chimney as the chimney sweep must clean it by working down from the top. The objects drawn at the end of the poem represent the tools of the chimney sweep's trade: a top hat (worn for luck), two brushes, a rope, and a fifteen-pound weight.

The following poem is a class collaboration by fifth and sixth graders in Ballard, one of the older sections of Seattle.

CHIMNEYS

Like buildings upside down
or wells,
square and round, rectangular,
cannons firing straight upwards!
They have long necks and dunce caps at the top,
heads with hats of slate
or crowns,
they wear soot coats
and brick shoes.
The fireplace is the rib-cage of the house
with the heart inside.
At the top of the chimney
stringy like snakes
shapes imitating chimneys, funny people—
in the winter you walk down the sidewalk
watching little puffs of breath
above each person,
spray-mist like fog;
you sink down in your coat
not to let all the heat out.
People have brick coats and lead socks,
moving chimneys.

    —Whittier Elementary School, Mrs. Rearick's class

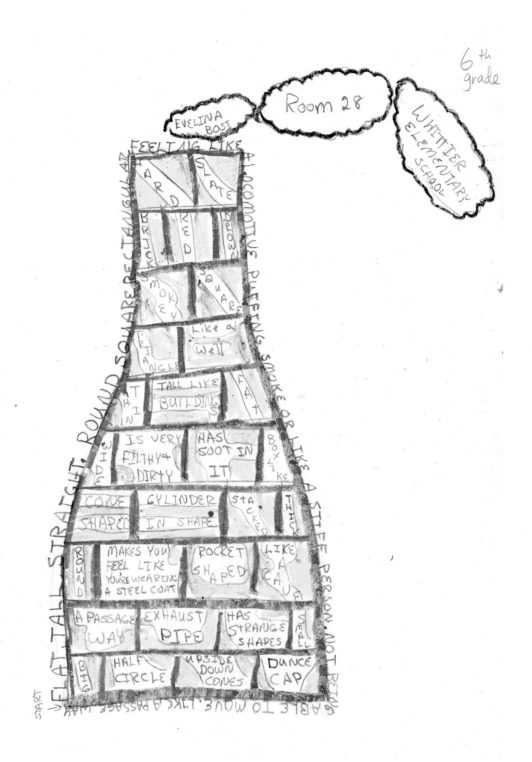

Evelina Bost

Room 28

6th grade

Whittier Elementary School

START FLAT, TALL, STRAIGHT, ROUND SQUARE, RECTANGULAR AT FEELING LIKE A LOCOMOTIVE PUFFING SMOKE OR LIKE A STILE PERSON NOT BEING ABLE TO MOVE, LIKE A PASSAGE WAY.

HARD SLATE

BRICK RED BROWN

SMOKEY SQUARE

BRICK ANGLE LIKE A WELL

THIN TALL LIKE BUILDING FAT

WIDE IS VERY FILTHY & DIRTY HAS SOOT IN IT BOX LIKE

CONE SHAPED CYLINDER IN SHAPE STACKED THICK

ROUND MAKES YOU FEEL LIKE YOU'RE WEARING A STEEL COAT POCKET SHAPED LIKE A CAGE

A PASSAGE WAY EXHAUST PIPE HAS STRANGE SHAPES SMALL

BIG HALF CIRCLE UPSIDE DOWN CONES DUNCE CAP

52

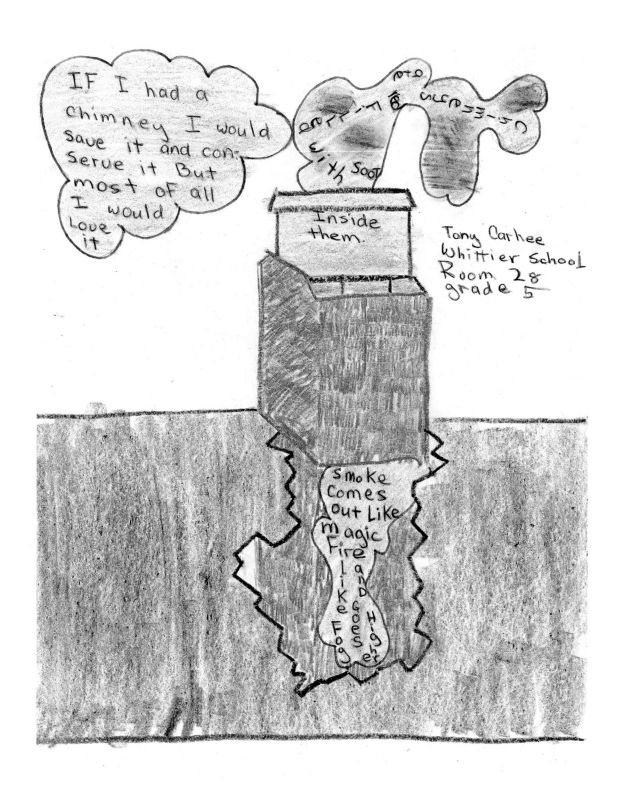

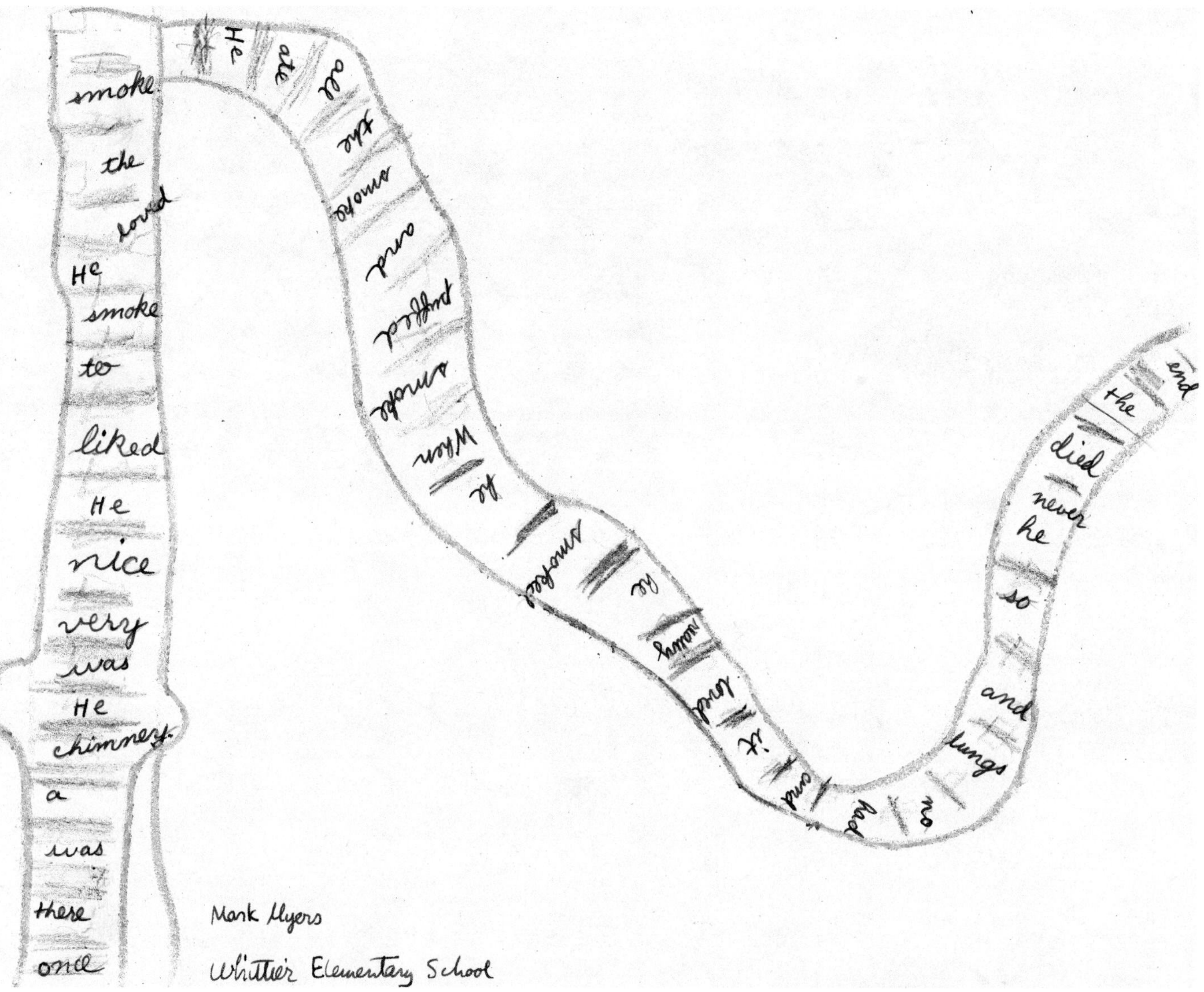

He ate the smoke and puffed smoke. When he smoked he had ... his lungs no ... and he died so he never died the ...

smoke the loved He smoke to liked He nice very was He chimney. a was these one

Mark Myers

Whittier Elementary School

By Gillian Anderson
R.9

start

My mother is a chimney sweep, that she is. chimmney sweeps are lucky, they get to get dirty without having to wash till the end of the day

but I have to clean every morning and night. But she has troubles too. She wears a big top hat for good luck so she does not fall off the top of the roofs. And she wears black clothes so nobody will know how dirty she really is. well, thats the end of my tale so farewell. 😊

55

Windows

The poems that follow were made in an older part of the city where many nineteenth-century buildings could be found, as well as churches with stained-glass windows. The variety of types of windows was surprising—they, too, were typical of many objects that surround us but which we rarely look at attentively. When we looked at a window, it would often become identified with the very act of looking. In the poem about a stained-glass church window, "Church bells ringing," the poet identified with the window itself, using the first person singular pronoun.

By: Ben Owen   Poetry   4th grade, University Heights
Elementary

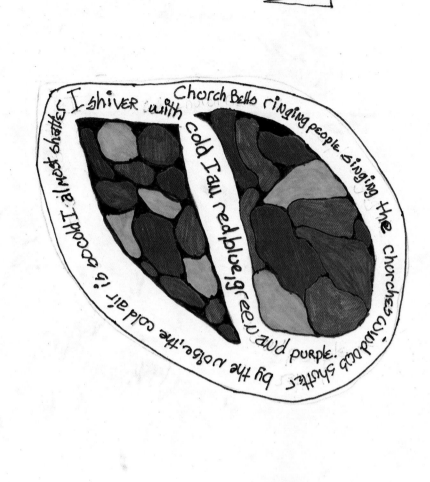

I shiver with Chorch Bells ringing people singing the chorches cwindows shatter by the noise, the cold air, it is so cold I almost shatter with cold I am red, blue, green and purple.

Andrea NICKEL
5th grade, University Heights

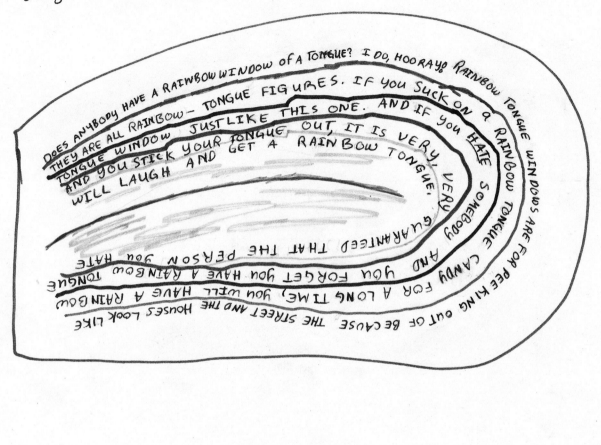

DOES ANYBODY HAVE A RAINBOW WINDOW OF A TONGUE? I DO, HOORAY! RAINBOW TONGUE THEY ARE ALL RAINBOW-TONGUE FIGURES. IF YOU SUCK ON A RAINBOW TONGUE WINDOWS ARE FOR PEEKING OUT OF BECAUSE THE STREET AND THE HOUSES LOOK LIKE CANDY AND YOU FORGET YOU HAVE A RAINBOW TONGUE FOR A LONG TIME, YOU WILL HAVE A RAINBOW GUARANTEED THAT THE PERSON YOU HATE SOMEBODY AND TONGUE WINDOW JUST LIKE THIS ONE. AND IF YOU HATE AND YOU STICK YOUR TONGUE OUT, IT IS VERY, VERY WILL LAUGH AND GET A RAINBOW TONGUE,

Dreams

Children often vividly remember their dreams. They enjoy drawing pictures of the most dramatic episodes in dreams, especially those that are recurrent. In dreams we express our most fundamental concerns, and although they may seem enigmatic, dreams are sometimes more intimate and forceful expressions of our emotions or anxieties than those produced by our conscious minds. Occasionally a student claims that he doesn't have any dreams, though that individual is likely to be one who has not explored (or been encouraged to explore) his memory of his dreams or given expression to his subconscious.

Some children said their dreams were hard to draw, that they could remember a feeling or emotion of a dream better than a visual setting. Many dreams are like this, and I often found it useful to speak of dreams in terms of the materials dreams are made of: Are they heavier or lighter than those of the waking world? Softer or harder, smoother or tougher? Is the dream world smaller or larger than the waking world, and which is more solid or more "real"?

Color

Colors do not correspond to emotions in any exact manner. Psychologists have done much research on the use of color by children, and it has proved impossible to link specific colors to specific emotions, something once thought possible—for example, red to anger, black to fear, green or yellow to jealousy. Children use colors in essentially the same way that adults use them. The language of art criticism applies to the use of color by both children and adults, and color is an extremely important element of expression. Similarly, inability to use it is often related to difficulties in other areas of expression.

Colors have value, intensity, and tone relations, both with respect to the color wheel and to one another; hues may be warm or cold.[1] Children sometimes use color in a haphazard way depending on those that are available and the cleanness (or dirtiness) of the color source, brush, or water. Yet color is very important and is most meaningful in its relation to the overall composition. Color will have an important function in each major area of the picture poem. It may be used for reinforcement or for contrast, for elaboration or compression, and may be applied to the total composition in some of the ways described in the discussion of integration on page 101.

When observing the composition of picture poems it is always apparent that the speed of composition immediately increases when color begins to be applied; often the color acts as a catalyst, giving rise to new thoughts, new shapes, and new words. In the picture poem color is associated not only with shapes and forms but also with specific words, syntax, and verbal meaning—this puts color into a much tighter and more ramified structure, expressing emotion, a state of mind, or an experience of the world. Sometimes the ideas for the specific colors to be used occur later in the process of composition (after the initial sketch and many of the words have been imagined), but once the colors are chosen, usually the whole design alters to accommodate them and form the final, overall composition.

The young people's use of colors was especially successful in their representation of dreams. Melanie Sutton's use of the stark black-and-white perspective in the poem "Nowhere" (p. 62), on the other hand, represents a statement about that particular nightmare and a conscious refusal of color. The green, blue, and black of the nightmarish monster on page 64 represents a fine use of "cold" colors, while the colors used in the rain poem on page 40 are warm and correspond to the "warm" feeling specifically described in the poem. Kristine Zitkovich's use of brown and gray to outline the guitar (p. 75) is a statement about the quality of the guitar's *sound* (the rounded outline of the guitar probably also suggested the notion that the guitar came "from the mountains"); and Portia Beard chose the color blue for a flute (p. 76), which may also be a statement about the quality of its sound. Far from being naive projections of feelings onto space, colors can be important tools in describing both psychological reality, the outside world, and the relation between them.

1. A good discussion of color can be found in *The Language of Drawing and Painting* by Arthur Pope (Cambridge, Mass.: Harvard University Press, 1949).

Averil Rothrock
4th grade

I was scared, I could hear my heart beat. It was dark. The only thing I could see was the shadows from the buildings around me. I could see the post with the name of the street but it was too dark to read it. I heard foot steps! I started to run, but where? It was a dead end street. Now I was really truly scared. I turned around to face my pursuer. It was Mr. Charles! Mr. Charles the policeman.

NOWHERE

Nowhere, nowhere, nowhere
But it's got to be somewhere,
I know.
It's just so different
Because it never suns, rains
or snows.

How can it be
That I got into
this place,
When there's
No door,
just lots of
space?
I looked to
My side,
Is there
someone here?
No, it's just
a mirror.
Nowhere.
Nowhere
Nowhere
Nowhere
Nowhere
Nowhere
Nowhere
Nowhere
Nowhere
Nowhere

By Melanie Sutton
5th grade

Mike Diehr

We found a cliff while we were exploring and we leaned over to take a look, and one of us leaned too far. He fell and twirled and down pounds and pounds down he went faster and faster farther and farther away smaller and smaller and smaller and smaller and smaller...

The badest thing I've ever seem. Green ugly, grouse and sharp blue and green monsters!

on DAYS
when the
sun is covered up
and most
is quiet
and
You're going
down a
water fall

and it's
like
You have nothing
to
do
But
go
down,
all
mistey

You
felt
like
just one
little Ball
going
down.

Richard

Palmason

5th grade

I had a dream that I was being attacked—attacked by a big, fat, drooly monster. Then I got out of bed and ran, far, and fast. I came to an iron wall and couldn't run anymore. The monster was about to bite me and—and I woke up.

Andrew Boudreaux
4th grade

Once, a giant hand reached out through the clouds. It picked me off the ship. The battleship started shooting at it and it dropped me. I tried swimming away but then I woke up. I was really scared.

James Hildebrandt
5th grade

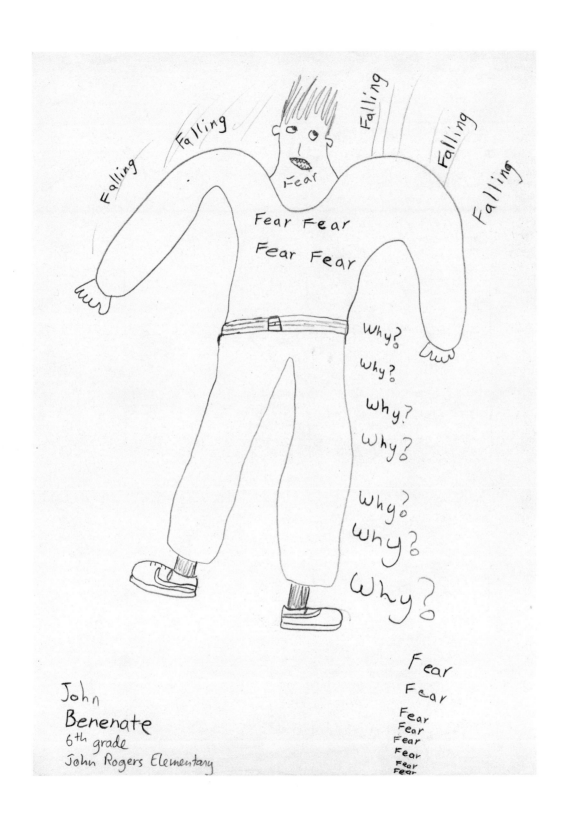

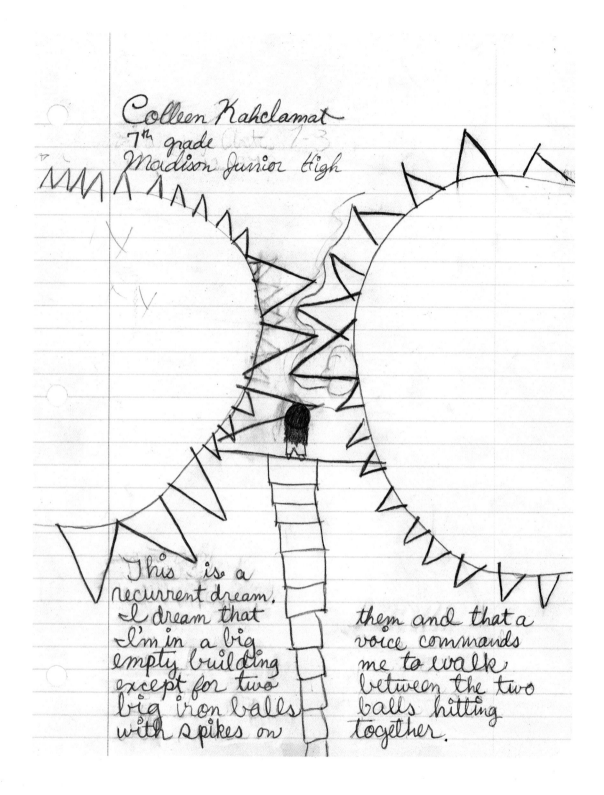

Colleen Kahclamat
7th grade
Madison Junior High

This is a
recurrent dream.
I dream that
I'm in a big
empty building
except for two
big iron balls
with spikes on

them and that a
voice commands
me to walk
between the two
balls hitting
together.

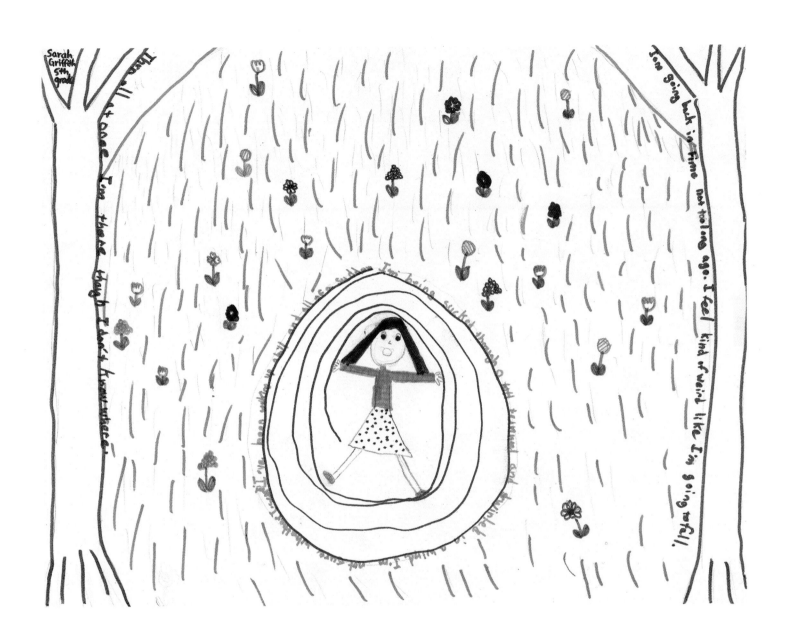

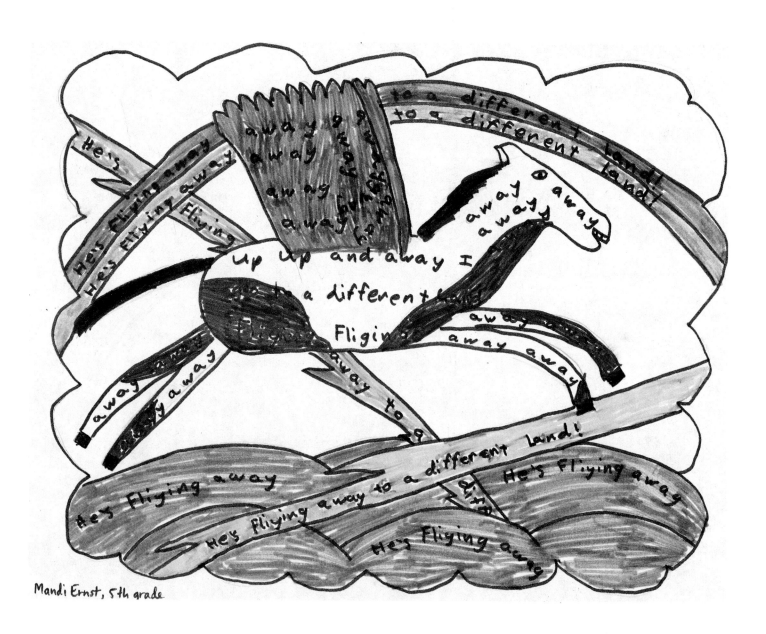

Mandi Ernst, 5th grade.

Sheila King
7th grade
Madison Junior High

as soon as I do I take you through my eyes. But as soon as I do I take you through that hurt my eyes. But as soon as I look looks like a tunnel I hope I'm going through a tunnel I hope I get through and a bunch of circles and circles and this world I'll come back and I go back to school and get I keep going, And when I get nowhere. But I'm here in my room and signals and 10 million

Sheila King

Musical Instruments

Musical instruments have very interesting, suggestive shapes that often excite the visual imagination. Many children play instruments; they enthusiastically volunteered to bring them to class and play sample melodies on each one. We could also look at them carefully and draw them. The sounds produced by the instruments presented a challenge to the ability of words to describe sensations. What words—what *mots justes*—could best account for an instrument's particular sound? This was also a challenge to our ability to use metaphors accurately, and we would ask ourselves questions such as: Can a sound be "fat" or "thin," can a sound be "big" or "small"? Do sounds have color, can they be red or black or dark? Are they rough or smooth—are they like surfaces, or textures? Can they be heavy or light— do they have weight? How much? Or are they like materials: like metal (brassy, for example), or like water, or sand? Can an instrument be said to have a personality?

Many fine adult poems have been written about musical instruments, for example Federico Garcia Lorca's "Guitar" and Jerzy Harasymowicz's "The Genealogy of Instruments." We enjoyed reading these poems in class, comparing them with observations and poems of our own.

We also wrote poems about other kinds of sounds not produced by musical instruments, for instance, the sound of wind or the steam whistle of a ferry. An exercise we did as a group was to write a class collaboration about the city "made of sounds" where we lived—we tried to render with words the most characteristic sounds we encountered every day.

Kristine Zitkovich,
5th grade

Portia Beard, 5th grade

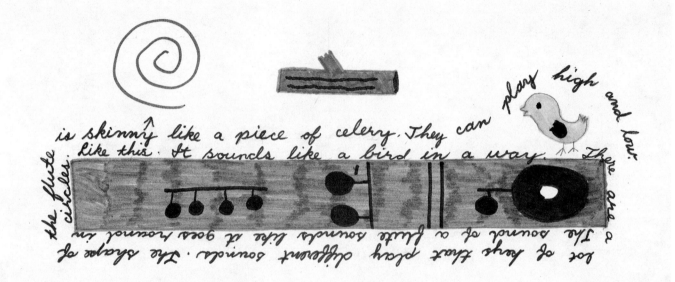

the flute circles.

is skinny like a piece of celery. They can play high and low.
like this. It sounds like a bird in a way. There are a

lot of keys that play different sounds. The shape of
The sound of a flute sounds like it goes round in

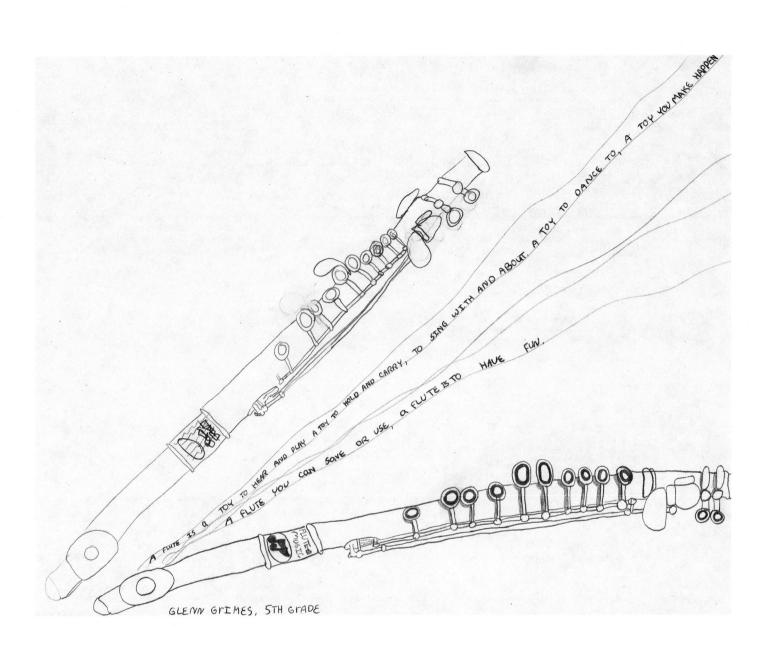

A FLUTE IS A TOY TO HEAR AND PLAY, A TOY TO HOLD AND CARRY, TO SING WITH AND ABOUT. A TOY TO DANCE TO, A TOY YOU MAKE HAPPEN A FLUTE YOU CAN SAVE OR USE, A FLUTE IS TO HAVE FUN.

GLENN GRIMES, 5TH GRADE

The wind sounds like a whistle   carried for
miles.
It sounds like bellows firing up the fire place,
It sounds like
moaning when it comes through your window
it's a high pitched whistle when it
forms a tornado.
the wind sounds great.

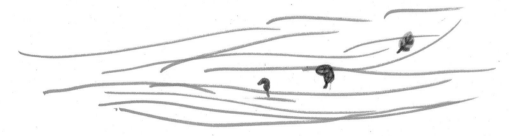

78

Nicole Meyer
4th grade
Montlake Elementary School

throwing food to them, swooping down and catching food in their mouth, the sun hot and bright makes the people come on the deck.

people throwing food to them,

When the ferry whistles, it's deep and loud the seagulls fly without a sound

79

Grapes

It is possible to make interesting poems about a great variety of spices, vegetables, or things that grow. They can become very sensual exercises using exotic colors (for example, eggplant in the shade or in the light), tastes, shapes (for example, ginger root), and visual sensations. The senses of children are remarkably vivid. Concrete poems can not only make use of the visual sense, but all of the senses can be brought to bear on the poem—odor, touch, taste, shape, as well as remembered sensory experiences from the past—all unified by the poem's final visual form.

The following poem was composed by a mixed group of fifth and sixth graders. The students then produced the picture poems on the next five pages.

GRAPES

Packed as tight as they can for juice
they are leaves about to turn color
or fresh water.
Shiny and smooth as a baby's new head
when washed by its mother.
The veins stream like tributary rivers
transparent on a stem with flowers, stem-tree.
Cloudy, with white snow hiding the shine
they are miniature watermelons or stars,
wet drops of rain—
piles of leaves.
They glow with light through them like raspberry sections
full as elevators
at rush hour taking people home.
They have the shape of the Solar System,
the Milky Way,
then this subway disappears
where whiteness hides the sheen
like powder or chalk
leaving only a tast of okra, taste of plums.

> —*Madrona Middle School (Darcy Sander,*
> *Anne Weisbrod, Michele Meaker, Meg Walker, Tina Thompson,*
> *Melissa McGrew, Robert Walker)*

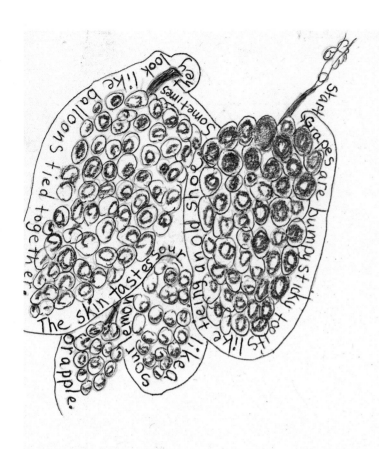

The text within the drawing reads:

Hey look like balloons tied together.
Sometimes
Grapes are bumpy sticky toots like Hemp and old shoes.
The skin tastes sour or apple.
sour lemon I liked

Danielle Gautreau
Stevens Elementary School, 5th grade

81

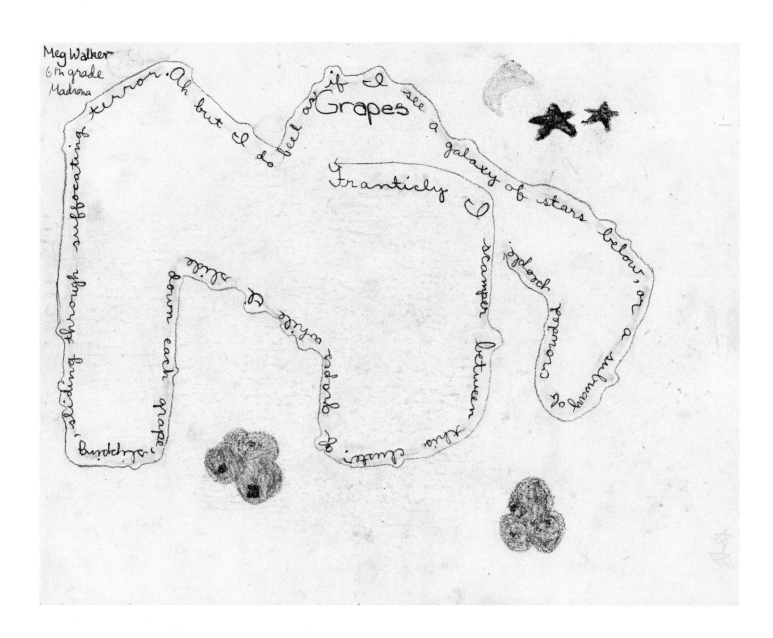

Meg Walker
6th grade
Madrona

Grapes

Ah but I do feel as if I see a galaxy of stars below, or a suffocating terror.

Franticly I scamper between this cluster of grapes which are sliding through suffocating terror, squelching, down each grape slide.

Darcy
Sander
6th grade
Madrona

Grapes

Many Grapes come to invade
the Earth, they came in great
Bunches Like people in crowded
elevators, They feel like mud
to our army's feet. Their shapes
are like that of a Milky Way. When
explosions come up behind them
you can see their veins, They
look like tributaries to rivers.
Some grapes look like our
oval egg like people,
While others look like
beings from outer
space. Some
Cannibals eat them
I wish they
were our
Friends.

Portia Beard
5th grade

the grape looks like a Big dome

a grape is shaped like a egg

the seed inside looks like a rock

grapes are greenish and redish color

they're very juicy and sweet

they come in all sorts of shapes

grapes look like a miniature watermelon

grapes have a white sheen over them

the seed inside the grape looks like a pupil

grapes are skinny and fat

a grape looks like a Balloon

the seed looks like a spaceship

if a grape stood up it would lean Back and fo

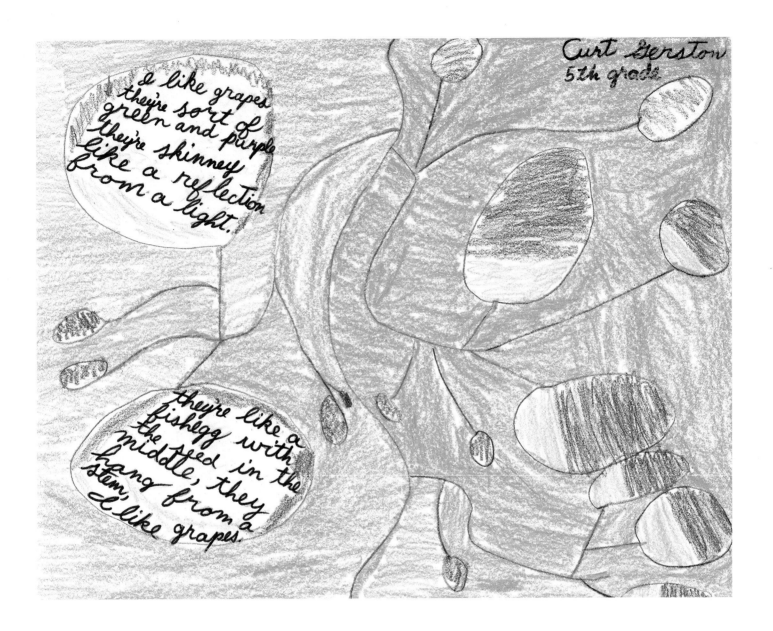

Pomegranates

Pomegranates have very suggestive shapes and, like roofs, appeal to the visual imagination. Their season is short, but in November and early December they can be brought into the classroom where they have a unique ability to help provoke metaphors. The effect of the seeds, and the tunnels where they are packed, is very different when the pomegranate is sliced lengthwise from when it is sliced crosswise. Although pomegranates are suggestive, they are not easy to describe; they present a challenge to one's verbal ability. Because people tend to see in them what they want to see, they serve as a kind of Rohrshach test.

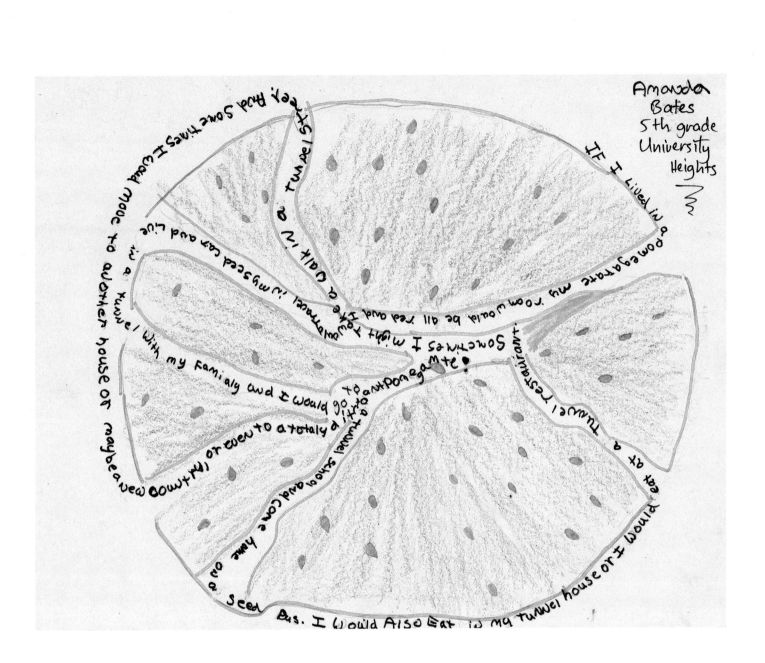

Amanda
Bates
5th grade
University
Heights

IF I lived in a pomegranate my room would be all red and like a quail in a tunnel I might jump around in myself or and live in a tunnel with my familay and I would go to a pomegamte. Sometimes I might Tournament restaurant a tunnel restaurant or I would eat in my tunnel house or I would eat at a tunnel restaurant Bus. I would Also Eat in my tunnel house or or a seed Bus or even to a totaly different school and come home or (Af+moon or even to a totaly different home or maybe a new with my Family and I would go to a pomeganate. Sometimes I might Tunnel with my familay or maybe a new to another house or move to another house or maybe I would move to another house Street And Sometimes I would move in a tunnel

87

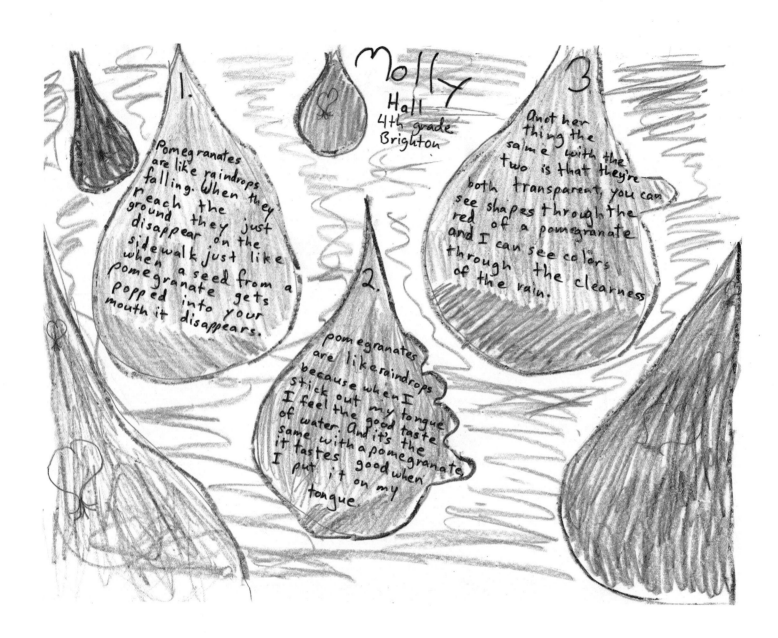

Molly Hall
4th grade
Brighton

1. Pomegranates are like raindrops falling. When they reach the ground they just disappear on the sidewalk just like when a seed from a pomegranate gets popped into your mouth it disappears.

2. pomegranates are like raindrops because when I stick out my tongue I feel the good taste of water. And it's the same with a pomegranate, it tastes good when I put it on my tongue

3. Another thing the same with the two is that they're both transparent, you can see shapes through the red of a pomegranate and I can see colors through the clearness of the rain.

Hank
Breeding

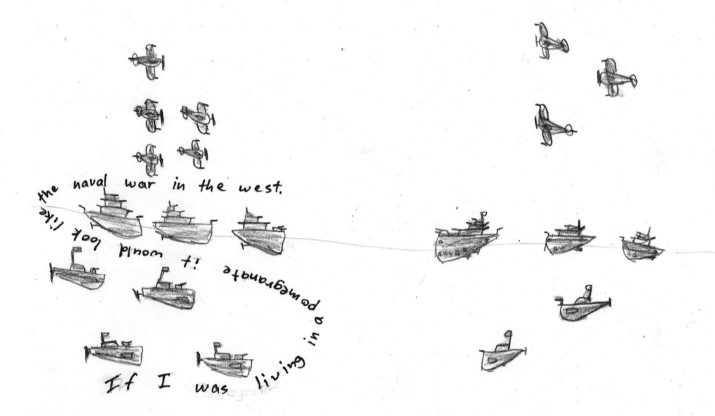

the naval war in the west.

If I was living in a pomegranate it would look like

89

Mountains

Sometimes I was fortunate and it was possible to see high mountains from the classroom, or large expanses of water and passing ferries. Especially at the secondary level students have a very strong feeling for nature and an impulse to project their feelings upon it, particularly where natural forces can be seen in impressive forms. Often mountains have Indian myths associated with them, for example Mount Rainier and the Oympics. We were able to discuss these myths and see in a precise, graphic way from the classroom window where some of the actions of a myth took place. For example, from a West Seattle classroom window we could see the deep gashes of ravines in Mount Walker just above Jackson Cove on the Hood Canal; these were said to be scratches made during a fight between a snow-clad female deity and her husband.[2]

The graphic techniques used in these mountain poems are quite varied. In some the written line of words resembles a smooth contour, in others a jagged, rocky silhouette. One poem has no drawn lines at all, only lines of words mimicking shapes. And one poem, beginning "Snow upon the mountain tops," is written inside the sun.

2. Ella Clark, *Indian Legends of the Pacific Northwest,* (Berkeley: University of California Press, 1953), p. 30.

In daytime
Let your Gaze Stray upwards and See brown trunks leafy green leaves
And white capped mountains Then watch the sunset settle
over the white capped mountains turning them yellow
orange and red then watch the black night move in
making everything very silhouettey. Blackest
black, only
the faintest
ray of light
Shows through
at dawn;
red, gold and
so on. Then
bright day
arrives

DLAxelson
ALene
7th grade, Madison Junior High

The mountains remind me Of rough water and they remind me of an EKG on the waves are it they go up and down jagged with some times white caps on the top of the waves. Like a heart beat

by Melinda Callow, 7th grade, Madison Junior High

John Fischer
7th grade
Madison Junior High

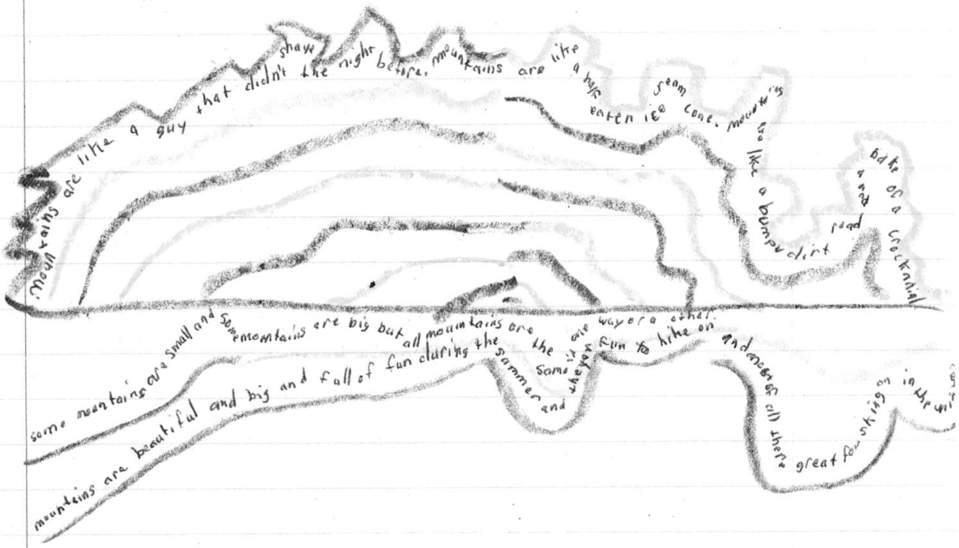

Mountains are like a guy that didn't shave the night before. mountains are like a big rotten ice cone. mountains are like a bumpy dirt road and like a crackanail bake of a

some mountains are small and some mountains are big but all mountains are the one way or a other. some they are fun to hike on and most of all there great for skiing in the winter mountains are beautiful and big and full of fun during the summer and

sue Green
7th grade
Madison Junior High

MOUNTAINS

START → THE MOUNTAINS ARE LIKE A SHARK, STEADY AND FIERCE SOMETIMES WHEN THE SNOW FALLS IT COMES DOWN LIKE POWDER ON YOUR FACE AS SOFT AS A CUSHION YOU CAN BOUNCE ON THE CUSHION AND BOUNCE UP AGAIN SNOW IS VERY OFTEN LIKE THE RAIN IN THE SKY OFTEN FALLING MANY MANY TIMES NOW WE'RE DOWN HERE ON THE CANAL WHERE THE WATER SPLASHES AND FLOWS LOTS OF TIMES) SOMETIMES IT EVEN SINGS TO US SOFTLY AND SWEET LIKE THE FOREST AND THE TREES.

Snow upon the mountain tops. Inside the forest thoughts. Snow melts in the forest peek thinks ground, and the snowy peek thinks the ground, and in the Sound.

Patrick Allen
7th grade
Madison Junior High

Myths—*The Creation*

Many myths and legends are stories. Poems can tell stories, but if they are too complex—if there are many episodes or characters, or if dialogue is important—it is best to treat them with prose. Some myths, however, have a strikingly visual character and can be successfully treated as poems. The numerous creation myths are very suggestive visually; there are at least a dozen related creation myths in Northwest Indian mythology alone, all of which have Raven as a leading character. They are dramatic, vivid, and appeal to both the visual and verbal imagination.

The biblical genesis is somewhat less pictorial with its fiats, but it is also more familiar to most students, and some fine poems have been made on that theme. Many teachers and school administrators choose to avoid such material for fear of offending the religious sensibilities of parents. This is unfortunate, since much of the finest art in Western Civilization—especially from the Renaissance and earlier—treats religious themes. Eliminating all religious material from the curriculum would mean throwing away a great deal of valuable culture; for that matter, many non-Judeo-Christian myths and legends comprise essential parts of the religious beliefs and cosmologies of different cultures. Treated sensitively and respectfully, they can give rise to striking poems.

Once there was only darkness. Raven knew this and wanted to change it. One day Raven learned where the sun and moon and stars were kept. He set out to get them from a Miser's house at the end of a river. When he got there he changed himself in to fire and set the house on fire. The miser ran out of the house and Raven took the sun, moon and stars. Raven threw them up in the sky where they now stay.

MIKE DIEHR 5th grade

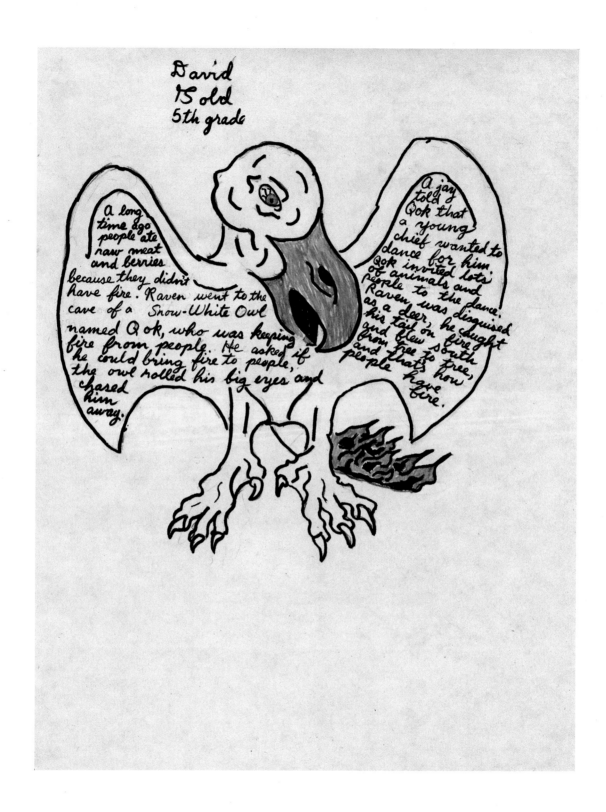

David
15 old
5th grade

A long time ago people ate raw meat and berries because they didn't have fire. Raven went to the cave of a Snow-White Owl named Qok, who was keeping fire from people. He asked if he could bring fire to people, the owl rolled his big eyes and chased him away.

A jay told Qok that a young chief wanted to dance for him. Qok invited lots of animals and people to the dance. Raven was disguised as a deer, he caught his tail on fire and flew south from tree to tree, and that's how people have fire.

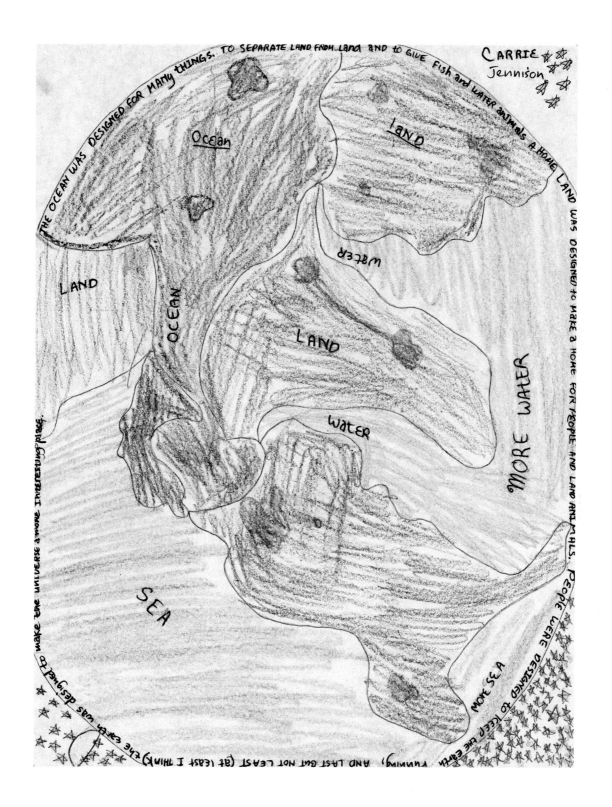

THE OCEAN WAS DESIGNED FOR MANY THINGS. TO SEPARATE LAND FROM land AND to GIVE FISH AND WATER animals A HOME. LAND WAS DESIGNED to MAKE a HOME FOR PEOPLE AND LAND ANIMALS. PEOPLE WERE DESIGNED TO KEEP THE EARTH running, AND LAST BUT NOT LEAST (at least I THINK) THE earth was designed to make the universe a more interesting place.

CARRIE
Jennison

Ocean

LAND

LAND

OCEAN

LAND

WATER

WATER

MORE WATER

SEA

MORE SEA

99

ANDREA NICKEL

100

Integration

It is impossible to measure integration in any exact manner; certainly it cannot be measured numerically. Art resists quantitative measurement, and this is probably its greatest strength: the final evaluation must always be made by an individual, and will always reflect that person's own unique judgment. However, it could be useful to list a few features which may be present in a composition, or may be absent.

—Continuity between verbal and visual elements. The meanings of the words mimic or echo the lines, taking them into account in some way (there is a great variety of ways of doing this), not ignoring them.

—The visual and verbal media may be applied anywhere on the white space of the paper. The relationship between the two media need not be merely horizontal, as with the written "line," but may be established in any orientation: above, below, coming together at an angle, sideways, etc.

—Continuity may be expressed not only by choice of word or metaphor, but by the use of phrasing, syntax, and punctuation.

—Continuity of word and shape. The placement of words may take into account not only the lines (or outlines), but also shapes and their areas on the paper, as well as what these shapes represent in nature.

—The senses. Objects can be dealt with by all the senses, and attributes of these objects can be rendered visually as well as verbally.

—Color. The use of color may reinforce both visual shapes and verbal meanings. Words dealing with color, and colors themselves, may describe objects and forms but may also express attitudes, feelings, emotions, and the imagination.

—Repetition. Continuity applies not just to one isolated space in the composition, but a pattern is repeated in one way or another throughout. One form, as well as verbal meaning, gives rise to another, which in its turn generates another, and so on. Sometimes this repetition results in increasing abstraction, or stylization. Any portion of the paper has the potential to be used for either drawn shapes or written words, and once the composition is begun, any segment of the white space can be used to carry the meaning forward—an inch away, or three, or even ten inches away. As with paintings, "analogies" may be distributed anywhere within the frame. The teacher must be extremely alert to these, and must be constantly aware of the possibility that one term of the analogy may be verbal, the other term visual.

—Contrast. This repetition may take the form of contrast or opposition. Visual shapes may be contrasted with one another, as well as verbal meanings. Or a visual shape may serve as "punctuation" to contrast two very different kinds of verbal statement.

—Breadth of space. Objects are observed attentively, not only the near but also the far. The students should be encouraged to relate different areas of experience to one another, above all to discover the analogies that exist *in their own experience*. This requires recall and the activation of memory. Even with the very young, if their memory is not activated space will seem flat, shallow, and there will be great poverty of analogies in their composition. For example, in poems about roofs and chimneys, students should be asked if they have seen similar objects anywhere else, perhaps in other cities or during vacation trips. Experiences should not be kept separate simply because they occurred in different places, at different times, or with different people.

—Amount of personal participation. This is a broad category, but it is difficult to describe any object accurately without introducing comparisons from personal experience. If this experience cannot be brought to bear, along with the imagination, the more objective rendering usually suffers also. An alert use of the senses will fuse the two.

—Proportions. Proportions can be expressive and related to contrast. The proportions of shapes to one another (as well as the words treating these shapes) and to the overall area of the page and its edges serve to distribute meaning and confer importance.

—Variety. Some compositions which make use of very few elements are often the most effective; this in itself is a type of selection or variety. On the other hand, a variety of techniques can be used in one composition, and this can be very enjoyable.

—Depth, perspective, shading. These elements are usually first used in the sixth grade or later. They can add greater solidity to space, and they, too, can be combined with words.

4 / Seventh Grade to High School

The ability to think verbally and visually at the same time is one of the most striking traits of children between fourth and seventh grades, but it is never a static equilibrium. Aptitude in the language arts steadily increases, as does the ability to draw and paint. Space is convincingly rendered in these poems, sometimes mingled with subjectivity in a playful manner and with humor, which is a sign of objectivity or balance—this humor is often rejected later on, however, in the eighth and ninth grades. Children aged nine to thirteen direct their attention toward the outside world with great curiosity, and they have done so ever since the age of six or seven, throughout the stage sometimes referred to as "concrete operational."[1] They are constantly trying to master the diverse areas of life; objects and tools are manipulated according to various combinations, and there is a continuous testing of the borderline between the senses, the self, and physical reality. They are always moving outwards, and if in a poem they express subjective elements, these are usually frankly acknowledged. The poems express emotions and feelings, but they almost always arise from experience—from a concern for the world and acting in it, a certain extroversion. They are synthetic, expressing the desire to master the world by means of a mind-to-hand-to-eye coordination. Perhaps it could be said that this balance represents a greater degree of "objectivity" than any attempt to suppress the feelings of the individual when he is acting in the world, because it accepts these feelings in the name of realism.

The picture poem is an attempt *par excellence* to bring the individual into synchronization with outside reality, using all his senses and treating them as a unified whole. Children at this stage differentiate quite well between the inside and outside worlds. What is called animistic thinking has been left behind by the age of ten. Space is spontaneously grasped and naturally dependent on the senses which perceive it; this balance between the individual and the outer world is so imperceptible that it almost goes unnoticed.

But later the balance becomes upset. The shift is accompanied by the acquisition of new skills. For example, in the sixth grade students learn perspective, their drawings become more realistic, they acquire the ability to use shading, and the individual line becomes more continuous, accurate, detailed. If there is more "realism" it is realism of a certain kind, what might be called fidelity to outer appearance. It is at this time—in the seventh and eighth grades—that color begins to disappear completely from their drawings. In the seventh grade color is still used but more sparingly, usually one or two colors in a picture poem at most.

1. Herbert Ginsburg and Sylvia Opper, *Piaget's Theory of Intellectual Development* (Englewood Cliffs, N.J.: Prentice Hall, 1979), pp. 161–68.

Crayons are avoided, colored pencils and pens are preferred, perhaps because of their sharper points. Although the ability to draw is impressive, it is not necessarily an activity seventh graders spontaneously enjoy. When asked how many enjoy drawing, almost all of the hands in a fourth, fifth, or sixth grade class will go up. In a seventh grade class the proportion will be considerably less, and in the eighth grade probably only about half the class, or less, will admit liking to draw. This does not mean at all that the quality is worse. Perhaps the greater complexity of their drawing impedes their spontaneity. Of course, adolescence begins at different ages: with girls it often starts in the sixth grade, with boys it may be two years later, and it is not possible to speak about grade differences with any great precision.

There is also an increase in verbal ability at this time as well as a tendency to make sharper distinctions between subjective and objective reality. Adolescents become more self-conscious—they have just had a sudden increase in their rate of growth after the slower rate of the preceding period. The notion of reality acquires much greater weight for adolescents partly due to the fact that they are changing. The new demand for realism is not only a demand for objectivity with respect to the outside world, but with respect to the self, one's identity. With greater self-consciousness comes the tendency to reject play as well as much of the mechanism of the free projection of feelings. The basic point of view, the earlier egocentrism, becomes more fragile with this self-consciousness, and the fusion of inner space and outer space is no longer so happy: the center of gravity shifts. The individual may identify with this newly grown body or may not. It is often a time of role playing, of questioning the self. What will they be in the adult world, and what will they do as men or as women, what will be their social function or profession, how will they be seen by others? The opinion of classmates becomes very important.

In the eighth grade and later in high school it is almost impossible to write class poems. Spontaneous oral expression does not work, and if forced, the results are usually inferior. Boys may begin to boycott poetry, even if they have high verbal ability, because of a new concept of a "male" role that might originate with the teacher, parents, or friends. The discipline problems of this period, too, may be due to the testing of roles, there is what is called role diffusion—they may over-identify with an image of a type of personality, perhaps someone from the world of popular music, film, or sports. They may project these images onto one another, and by seeing them thus reflected gradually clarify them. Related to this is a tendency to theorize, hypothesize, sometimes even to construct world systems.[2] On the intellectual level secondary-school students learn to develop a type of objectivity that requires them to abandon much of their former subjectivity in dealing with general concepts. In this sense space has become larger. But as there is often no color in their pictorial description of space, there is also uncertainty as to what image of themselves to project and integrate into that space. "Realism" easily becomes self-denying or defensive, a pretext for

2. Erik Erikson, *Childhood and Society* (New York: W. W. Norton, 1950), pp. 195, 231.

absence of self-expression. The importance of space becomes great, and the search for identity is also a search for space, even a definition of it. Space becomes dependent on this identity: the young man or woman is now *in* space, almost independent; the former stable vantage point is lost and the young person who takes the new role seriously is afloat in space without any support. He or she may simultaneously accept it and deny it, shy away from it. It is larger than ever before, it is available but has no solidity, it is very, very cold. What is more, there is no assurance that this stage will not continue unresolved into later life, and the adult world offers numerous examples of how the denial of space becomes permanent due to a variety of causes—specialization, the narrowing of horizons, self-limitation, or what the psychologist Erik Erikson has called ego restriction. Often space fails to give the adolescent a feeling of full richness; it lacks a necessary subjective element as if his own body were paradoxically left behind—he feels he must break through it by means of some strong sensation or action. Subjectivity is lacking and this causes frustration, anger. This is also at the origin of the special mordancy or "bite" in many poems by students in the eighth grade and high school, which gives them special appeal and strength.

The subjectivity is there, though perhaps somewhere that the adolescent cannot identify. It may be imprecise, not seeming to be in space at all: adolescence is a time of intensity of feeling, but the feeling is often disembodied, not assigned to a concrete object. In student writing this subjectivity often takes the form of sentiment that seems stronger than the context merits—sadness about the sun going down, happiness at the sound of a musical instrument or a bird or the ocean, a passion for horses, longing, or idealization. In poetry there is an appreciation for rich rhyme at this age. Younger children frequently enjoy rhyme but more as a game, as a display of skill or as a mnemonic device, than as expression; or if a teacher has stressed rhyme, the student may expect poems to rhyme. But in adolescence the richness of rhyme, its sonorousness, is appreciated, and sometimes almost everyone in a class will rhyme enthusiastically.

In junior high school the verbal part of a picture poem will often pull away from the visual part. Each may have a tendency to develop a momentum of its own—when the student starts to write the verbal part of a picture poem, he may write intently until it is finished, then the visual part will be elaborated at the very end. Occasionally the words and shapes will seem to retreat from one another, the visual shapes being large and open, the words small, cramped, hard to read. But usually the students sense that although they are working in two media which are different, still both *could* come together, and they accept the promise that the two can be combined or integrated. It does not happen easily, but the goal is sensed, it seems necessary almost like a polar attraction. When verbal and visual elements come together, they have the strength of a sudden connection, as if overcoming resistance. Space is larger than ever before, and so is the inner world; to put them together now requires struggle as well as spontaneity, but the rewards are very great.

Pomegranates

In the following picture poems inspired by pomegranates, as well as in subsequent groups of poems in Chapter 4, it should be noted that seventh graders used color sparingly, while eighth and ninth graders used no color whatsoever. As the authors advance in age, color seems to drain from their picture poems. Often I would remind students that colors were available and point to an opened box of colored pencils, felt-tip pens, or crayons on a table, but frequently these would go begging. The students were most willing to add color when they could take their poems home after school and work on them in privacy. A poem by seventh grader Shaun Berkbigler retains some color, and begins with the words, "I must be in Eden"; Berkbigler had read many books by J. R. R. Tolkien.

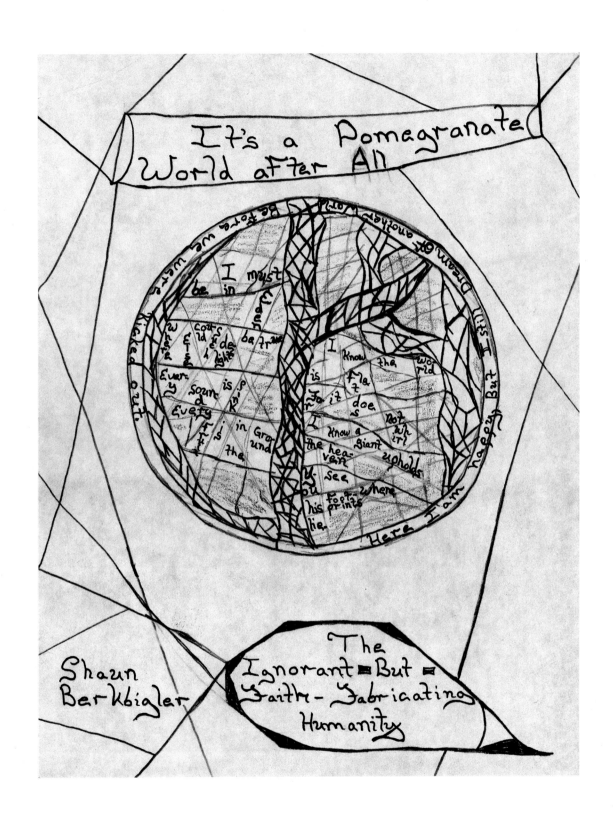

It's a Pomagranate World after All

I must be in Heaven be from could de light Every sound is where I fell out. I know in Ground it the Every If it is

Dream of another World

Before we were here

I know the world is so it does not with it! I Know a Giant upholds the heaven If you See where his foot-prints lie.

Here I am happy But It is

Shaun Barkbigler

The Ignorant - But - Faith - Fabricating Humanity

107

Dawn Detwiler
8th grade
Monroe Junior
High

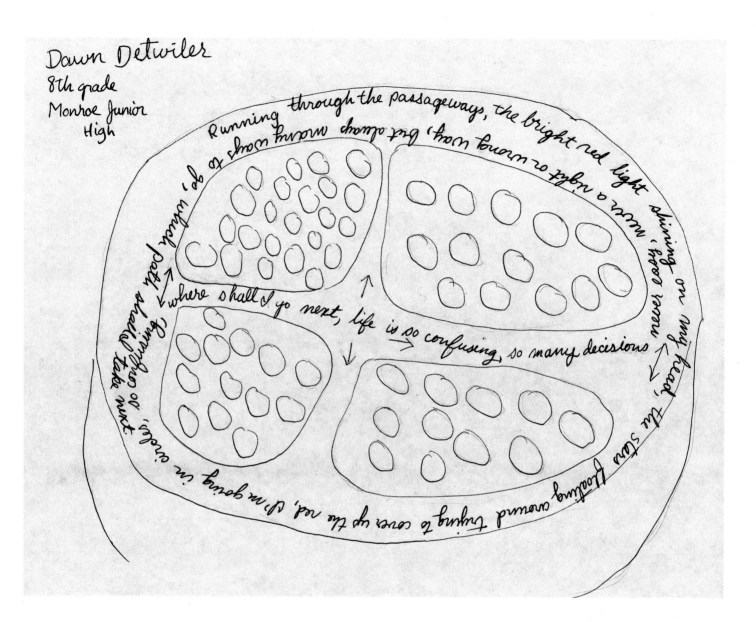

Running through the passageways, the bright red light shining on my face, never can I find or know which way to go, which way, but always which path should I take next, where shall I go next, life is so confusing, so many decisions floating around trying to sore up the sed, I'm going in circles.

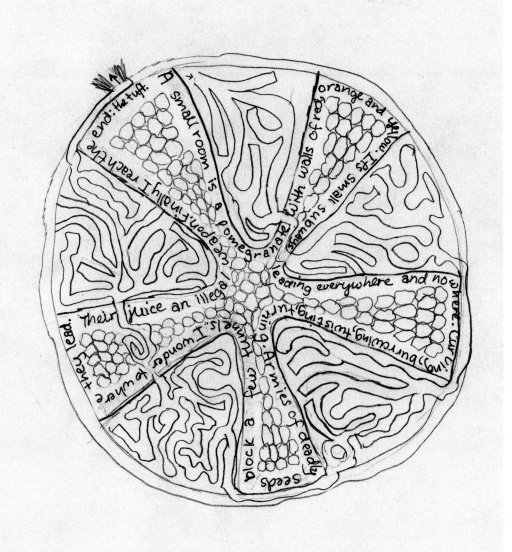

Beth Van mappes 8th grade Eckstein Middle School

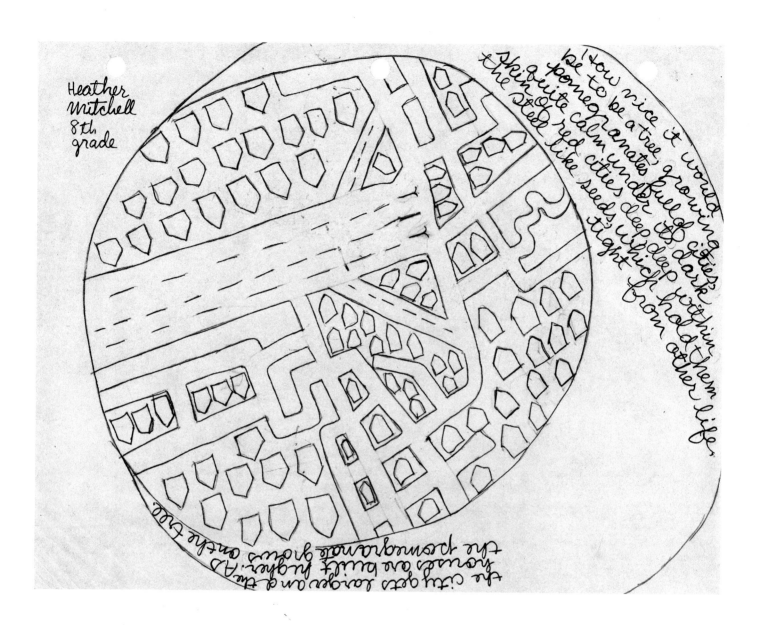

Heather
Mitchell
8th
grade

How nice it would be to be a tree, growing
pomegranates, full of cities within them,
skintite calm under its dark within
thin soft red cities deep, which hold them life
the seeds tight from other life.

the city gets larger and the AD
houses are built higher.
the pomegranate grows on the tree.

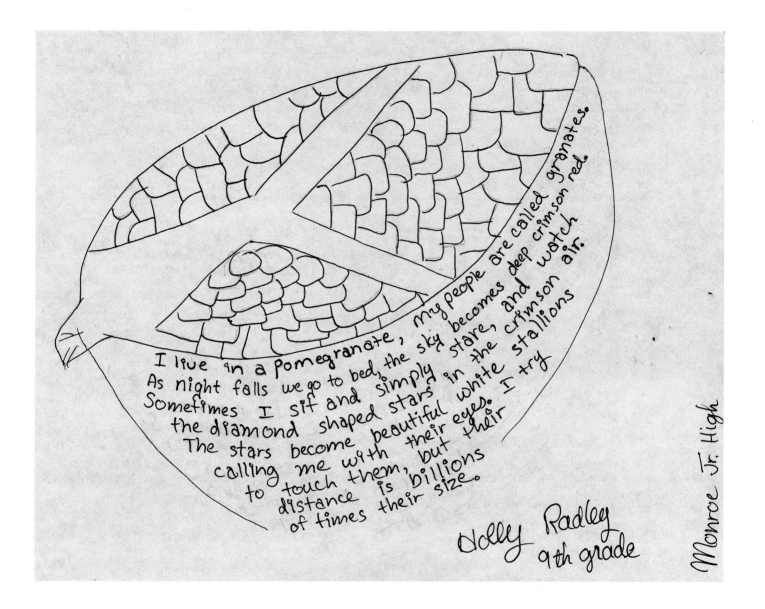

I live in a pomegranate, My people are called granates.
As night falls we go to bed, the sky becomes deep crimson red.
Sometimes I sit and simply stare, and watch the crimson air.
the diamond shaped stars in the white stallions I try
The stars become beautiful their eyes. I try
calling me with their eyes. but their
to touch them, is billions
distance of times their size.

Holly Radley
9th grade

Monroe Jr. High

111

Rain

It is interesting to compare the poems by older secondary school students on rain with the poems by primary school students that we have already seen in Chapter 2. Although considerable freedom is taken in the direction of line, there is greater caution in the older students. The lines tend to form small groups of two or three or more with the same general shape, the individual line being less independent and adventurous. An overall visual symmetry is often imposed on the poem, and this reflects the manner of composition, the visual and verbal parts done in different steps, not simultaneously. The words, however, may sometimes achieve a greater poignancy and a deeper, rawer personal note than before.

Christine Leray
8th

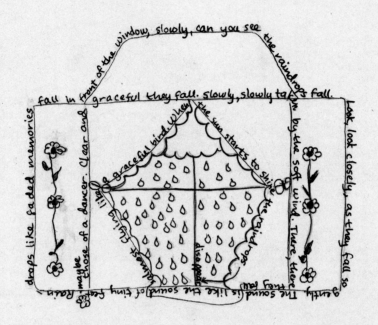

Carrie Barbee
8th

rain is like a small child's mind a constant pitter patter running over and over hundreds of times

you never know when it will come of it but someday you'll know where on the

over hills and fields it may stay short and forests

or it may spray a very well when it comes

but so wear it a very very long time

In several of these poems a strong sentiment is present that is only partly attached to an object. The next group of poems (beginning with Ingrid Weisenbach's "Suddenly the sun goes down . . . ," p. 117) might be called romantic in this sense—often the emotion of loneliness or happiness does not have a specific concrete setting or cause, and this is part of the very nature of the particular emotion or state of mind. The use of a visual space and structure helps give form to the poems.

Of course, adults frequently express this kind of emotion. A feeling that is dissatisfied, discontented, or simply lyrical overflows the boundaries of its immediate setting and is projected against space. Sometimes it lacks self-consciousness, or its origin is not acknowledged; still, it is no longer a spontaneous projection of the senses on a given setting or object, as in the poems by younger children. Instead, the emotion overwhelms this immediate, concrete setting, coming from a different, subjective source and altering both the setting and space as a whole.

Coupled with the presence of strong feeling, disembodied or diffuse, is a more direct kind of revolt. The earlier sense of play implied a balance of freedom and acceptance, and avoided a head-on clash. Revolt in the seventh and eighth grades, and later, might still include playfulness, but this will acquire a new causticity and irony. Poems about myths, legends, and the creation written by junior-high-school students are often full of fantasy and whimsical feeling, but the next three—"When God created the sun," "In the beginning," and "The Big Bang Theory"—are characteristic of three different types of revolt: feminist, mocking or blasphemous, and scientific. In the first, God the creator is a woman with long, elegant, bright red fingernails, who forms the ball of the Earth. In the second, the process of creation is reduced to ironic daily notes on a dime store calendar. In the third, creation is the "big bang" postulated by Gamow, Burbridge, and others.

For many at this age, science satisfies the need for revolt because it provides a sense of realism and because it undermines many widely held traditions. It should be noted that all three of these poems that I call poems of revolt contain humor, and the revolt could be still more drastic.

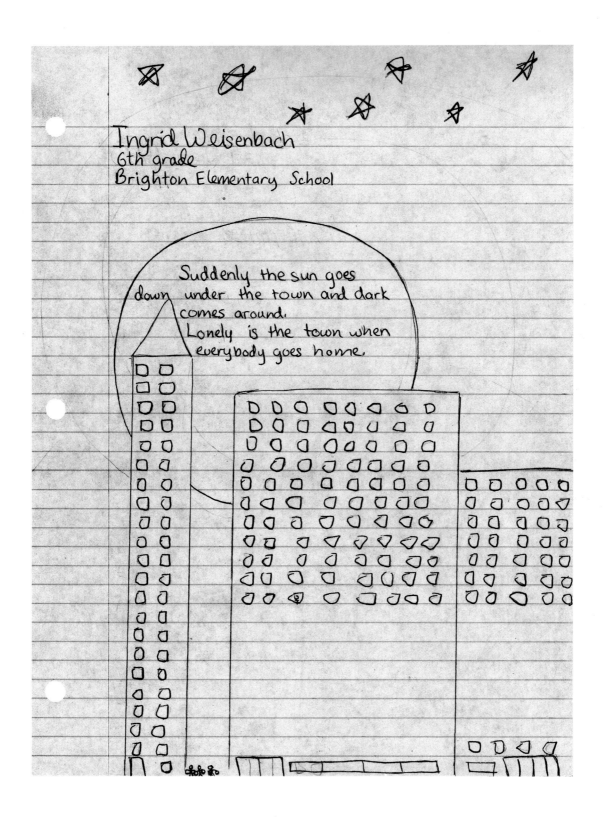

Ingrid Weisenbach
6th grade
Brighton Elementary School

Suddenly the sun goes
down under the town and dark
comes around.
Lonely is the town when
everybody goes home.

The sound
of the flute is
like the sound of
a butterfly, yet also
like a running creek
as it passes over
rocks and logs.

The flute can
whistle with nature and
sing with the birds.

The flute is like the sound of
the rain on a warm
summer day.

The Flute

With every
note the flute
tells us of the
happy things in
life and assures us that
the bad will leave, and we will
be rewarded with good, happiness, and
the never ending joy . . . . . of the flute.

By Deanna
Storer 7th

Kelly Hawkins 7th Grade

Rain is the whispers of sorrow

The rain is gently falling like a baby's tears on my face. It whispers long ago, when the west wind was feared by all. The west wind is lost, then it tears to me and thinks again softly blowing its sorrowful tears in to me. It realizes all is lost, then sighs softly and the big a large gust of wind, then it stops sighs softly again. It begins fluttering and all is calm, then it sighs louder. Its big tears rain brushes against my face harder and sigh starts crying out to cry my face. Then it hit harder. Then it begins to cry harder and harder. It hit my face. Then it tells of sorrow to all the world. It crying loneliness and suffering begins to blame me for its suffering and tosses me around. Then it stops crying and gently blows, it sighs to me again...

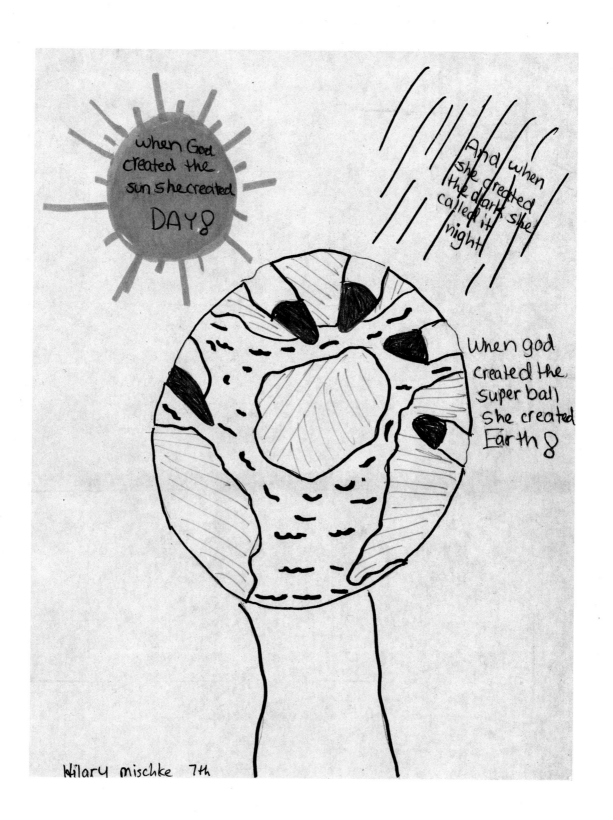

when God created the sun she created DAY8

And when she created the dark she called it night

When god created the super ball She created Earth8

Hilary mischke 7th

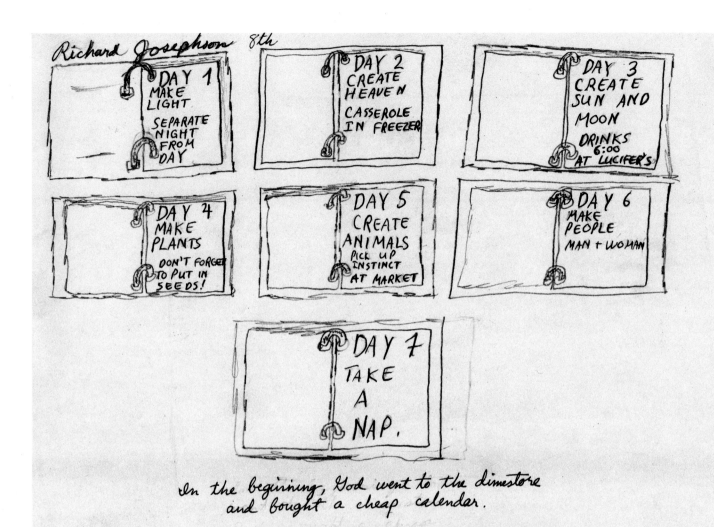

Richard Josephson 8th

DAY 1
MAKE LIGHT

SEPARATE NIGHT FROM DAY

DAY 2
CREATE HEAVEN

CASSEROLE IN FREEZER

DAY 3
CREATE SUN AND MOON

DRINKS 6:00 AT LUCIFER'S

DAY 4
MAKE PLANTS

DON'T FORGET TO PUT IN SEEDS!

DAY 5
CREATE ANIMALS
PICK UP INSTINCT AT MARKET

DAY 6
MAKE PEOPLE
MAN + WOMAN

DAY 7
TAKE A NAP.

In the beginning, God went to the dimestore and bought a cheap calendar.

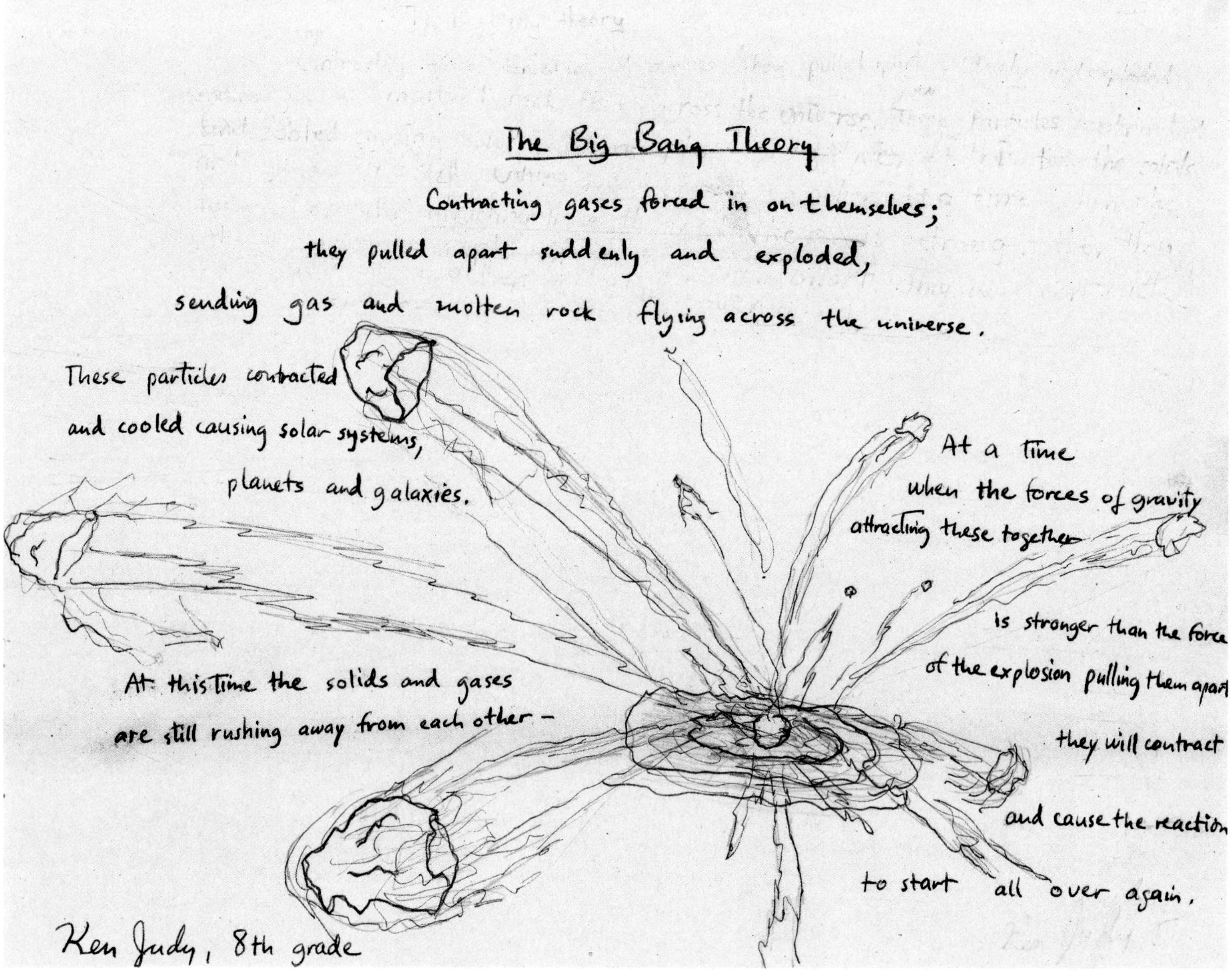

The Big Bang Theory

Contracting gases forced in on themselves;

they pulled apart suddenly and exploded,

sending gas and molten rock flying across the universe.

These particles contracted
and cooled causing solar systems,

planets and galaxies.

At a time
when the forces of gravity
attracting these together

is stronger than the force
of the explosion pulling them apart

they will contract

and cause the reaction

to start all over again.

At this time the solids and gases
are still rushing away from each other —

Ken Judy, 8th grade

122

Realism

In the eighth grade and the years immediately following, the demand for realism in approaching the world becomes very strong, but at the same time there is the need to express intense subjective feeling, resulting in poems in which realism is thrown to the winds. These poems might be called realistic if we enlarge the term to include the reality of the feeling, thinking individual. It is interesting to look forward and compare the particular sense of realism encountered at this age with that in adult poems (Chapter 5), and to look back at the sense of realism expressed by the younger children. The concept of realism, of what is real and what is not, is different in each of the stages.

When we compare the poems by students between the ages of thirteen and eighteen with those by adults, it becomes clear that their demands of realism are in many respects even more stringent than those made by adults. The use of color as expression is held in tighter rein—or is more repressed—at this age than either before or after. The sense of play, or playfulness, is surprisingly developed in adult picture poems. Often we are unaware of the wide extent of adult "play" because we use other words for it. For example, comedy has a very large role in adult art and especially popular entertainment; this is largely anti-realistic and represents a widespread type of non-participatory adult "play." Sometimes this playfulness of adults is intellectual or based on parody, yet often it strikingly resembles the playfulness of children between nine and twelve years. But the visual shapes drawn by students from thirteen to eighteen years tend to be literally representational; usually they are less abstract or stylized than those of either older or younger poets. Less freedom is given to words to change their direction or shape; the space of the page is usually treated as inner or outer space but without rapid switches between the two. Projection is present but it is often insistent, monolithic, raised to a higher level of assertion.

When we look back at the use of play and humor in the poems by children between seven and thirteen included in Chapter 3, it is clear that they rarely confuse reality and fantasy in their play, and that humor is often used to distinguish between them. Occasionally it has been maintained that fantasy can be unhealthy for children and should be associated with autism,[3] but the play and humor that almost always accompany it—as in picture poems by adult poets and painters—make it a device for manipulation, for distinguishing the real from the unreal and integrating the two.

It is clear from the picture poems in this book that "realism" is not the goal or end product of the development from infancy to adulthood, far from it. On the developmental scale the human being does not progress from subjectivity to objectivity or realism—if he did, progress would equal repression and the complete separation of the psychological reality of the individual from the world surrounding him. Severe, often repressive demands of realism characterize above all the thirteen- to eighteen-year-old age group, and the basis for these demands is often highly subjective. As with the earlier play, they are frequently a device for testing, for probing the limits of reality. But now both inner and outer reality have become much larger, and the temptations to suppress one of them, or to keep them separate, are very great.

3. One of the strongest rebuttals of this view can be found in Bruno Bettelheim, *The Uses of Enchantment* (New York: Random House, 1976).

Amplifier, Pre-Amplifier, Power Supply

In the poems about the amplifier, pre-amplifier, and power supply it is possible to see in a highlighted form some of the fears of the adolescent age group, their frustrations and sense of fragmented reality. As with the poems about pomegranates, the electronic circuitry and tubes often evoked a feeling of stifling confinement. It is interesting to note that school was identified with both the pomegranate and the electronic objects in some examples. Yet in the following poems the family, city, and whole "outer" world are also brought into the process of dissociation. The last poem of the group, by Debbie Mackenstadt, probably expresses this best, where the body is compared to a puzzle that has been scattered all over space and is too difficult to put together.

The change to adolescence is accompanied by a disequilibrium which may last a shorter or longer time—it is open-ended and extends well into adulthood. No new stage of physical development will come to the aid of the individual; instead there is a longer period of integration into society—it is himself, and those who are near him, who must find this new equilibrium in society and "space." By then, however, artistic representation for most people will be an activity of the distant past. The skills of young adults in high school for manipulating language and visual forms are as well-developed as with many adults two or three times their age. Whether there will be further development is largely a matter of personal choice.

The selection of career or profession will affect this choice, and if verbal and visual skills are necessary for the career, development may continue. But more likely it will be verbal development, not visual. Already in early high school many young adults have part-time jobs, and frequently this coincides with the end of verbal or visual development. The situation of the young, growing high school students comes to resemble that of the serious artist: either they will continue this development by consciously pursuing their interest in art, or they will abandon both.

As for the integration of verbal and visual skills, this too depends on role or profession and generally falls victim to specialization. In colleges and professional schools courses usually separate the two, often rigidly. Their integration may take place in art, or in science, or in another field of endeavor, but it will largely depend on the individual, on his own resources and conscious motivation.

A final remark should be made about the developmental stages of children. They lead to physical maturity, but where does "development" lead in the domain of psychology, and of art? Traditions evolve, develop, but then are frequently discarded; the notion of progress in the arts has few adherents. Probably it is impossible to answer this question, as will be seen in the next section. The psychological concept of integration is attractive, but the question of selection—of which elements of reality are to be integrated—cannot be resolved. Nor can the question of where subjectivity ends and objectivity begins be answered in a satisfactory manner. A well-known psychoanalyst has written, "I know that all attempts to extract meaning from life are to a very large measure actually a projecting of meaning into life."[4] Piaget is of little help when studying artistic or cultural development. But above all when we consider the question of the relation of childhood to adulthood from a historical point of view, we see how biased we are.

Our own attitude toward children is not only widely different from our parents' and grandparents,' but immensely so once we push back into the early nineteenth century and beyond. The world which we think proper to children—fairy tales, games, toys, special books for children—even the very idea of childhood, is a European invention of the last four hundred years.[5] The words we use for young males—boy, garçon, knabe—were until the seventeenth century used indiscriminately to mean a male in a dependent position, and could refer to men of thirty, forty, or fifty. The word "child" expressed kinship rather than age. It is very rare to find children depicted as children before the beginnings of the modern world at the time of the Renaissance. Infancy, and a very high risk of mortality, lasted until the age of about seven, when the young man or woman became a small adult, was dressed like one, and shared the same games with adults, the same toys, the same fairy stories; they lived their lives together, not apart. We can trace the slow evolution of our modern concepts about childhood over the last four hundred years. The journey, though slow, was immense— it led to the development of a separate world of childhood. The new concept of childhood was adapted by the educationalists of the Renaissance, especially Erasmus, Vives, and Mosellanus; it became the stock in trade of the Jesuits, who were to dominate education in seventeenth-century Europe. The notion of childhood seems so natural to us, however, that it is difficult to conceive of any other state of affairs.

One of the major advantages of studying the different developmental stages of children and poetry is that it shows the wide variety of ways in which the human mind deals with space. The developmental context proves that we are in space, with a constant, dynamic relation to it. Like the cycles or evolution of style in art history, the study of the artistic rendering of space by children indicates an immense range of attitudes that vary from complete acceptance of space to complete denial. No attitude toward space can be exclusively "objective" or exclusively "subjective" because our relation to it must contain both elements, from the beginning of our lives to the end. With children as with adults, the creative act combines the two—combines the inner structure of the mind of the individual with the outer world surrounding him—in constantly changing forms.

4. Bruno Bettelheim, *Surviving* (New York: Alfred A. Knopf, 1979), p. 36.
5. J. H. Plumb, "Children, the Victims of Time," in *In the Light of History* (Boston: Houghton Mifflin, 1973), p. 153.

Liza Burke 7th

I am finally safe !!!!! The tubes were giant monsters about to crash down on me. It was scarey. The tubes were their glass walls. I walked toward it. It was sky scrapers. They were meant they were towering over me. The lights go out the lights in them monsters were dim suddenly change and looked like monsters staring back into skyscrapers. at me. Through

It was night I saw the city in the distance. But soon day light came. The lights

← Start

126

It was late at night, I saw the bottle city
in the distance glowing like a light bulb. I
started walking toward it and when I came to it
I tried to get in but it was blocked
off by the cork. I pu- lled and tugged but
it woul- dn't budge. I didn't
know what to do because my hotel
was inside there wasn't much air
left but fi n ally it
opened.

Hotel

rawled

ide. It

was very quiet.

Hilary Mischke

127

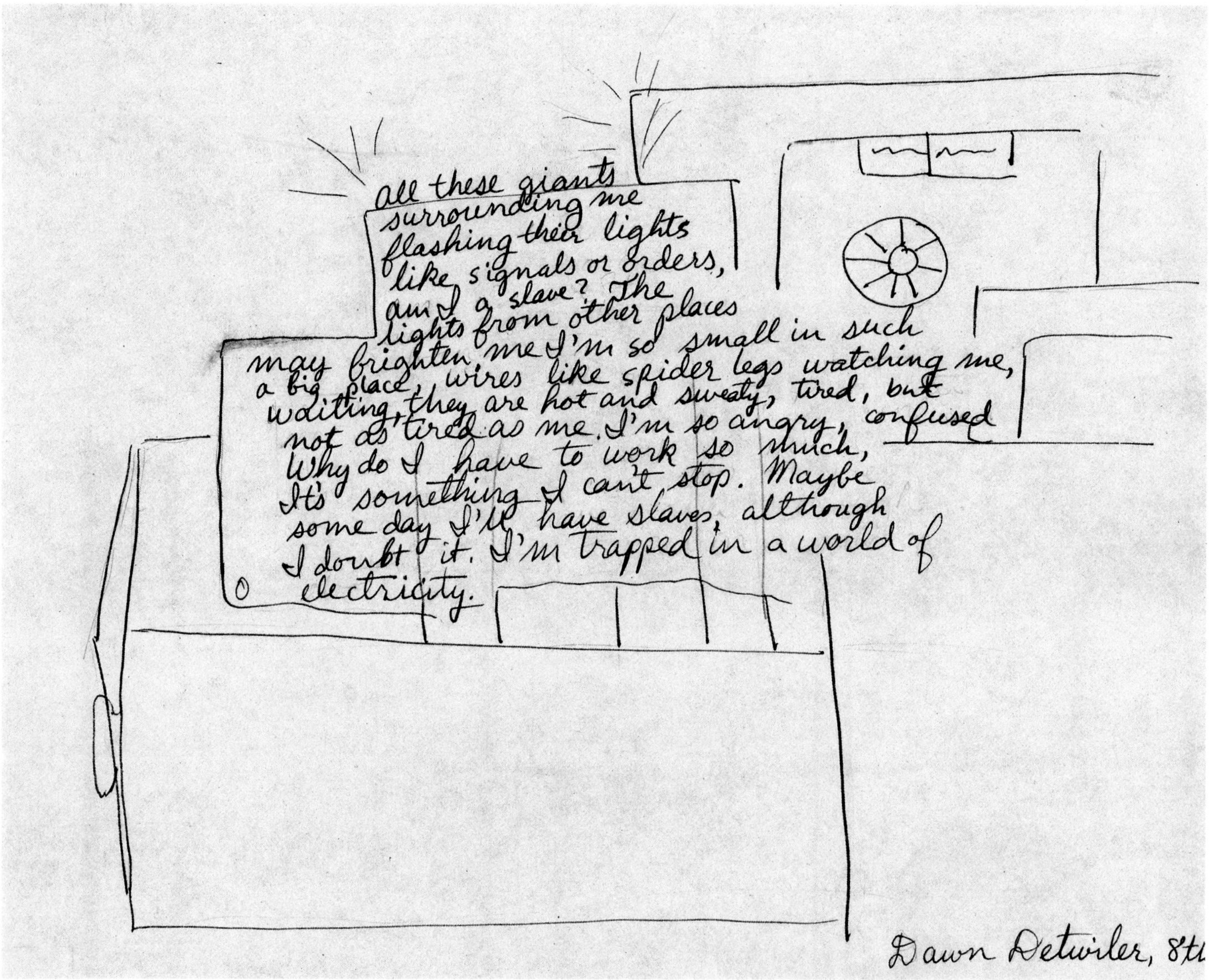

all these giants
surrounding me
flashing their lights
like signals or orders,
am I a slave? The
lights from other places
may brighten me I'm so small in such
a big place, wires like spider legs watching me,
waiting, they are hot and sweaty, tired, but
not as tired as me. I'm so angry, confused
Why do I have to work so much,
It's something I can't stop. Maybe
some day I'll have slaves, although
I doubt it. I'm trapped in a world of
electricity.

Dawn Detwiler, 8th

128

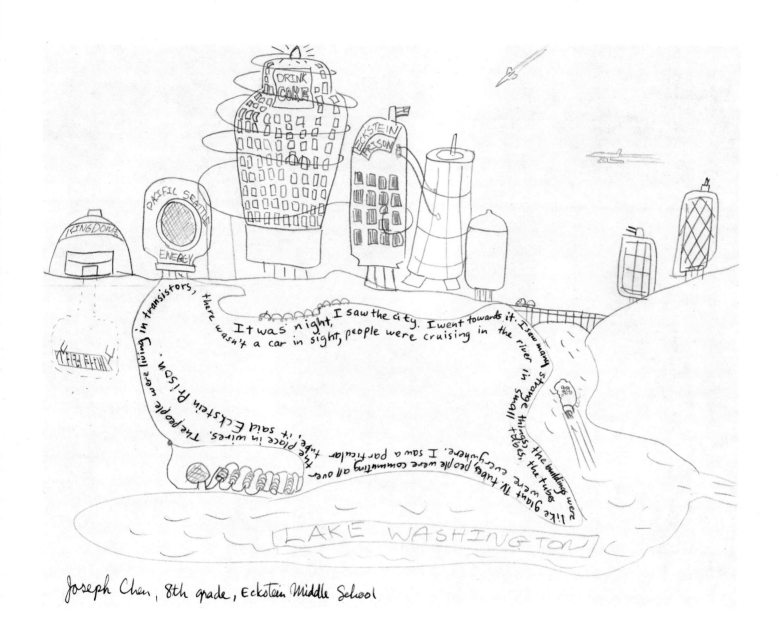

Joseph Chen, 8th grade, Eckstein Middle School

I feel like a puzzle that is scattered all over,
too difficult to put together
or not enough time—

I have too much to do,

and not enough time to do it.

Debbie Mackenstadt
10th grade
Nathan Hale High Schoo

130

5 / Adult Art:
The Combination of Verbal and Visual Forms

Many of the works by poets or painters combining verbal and visual elements have been produced during the twentieth century, often by members of avant-garde artistic movements. However, this statement is partly misleading for two reasons. Poets and artists such as Guillaume Apollinaire, André Breton, or Joan Miró, though at one time considered "avant-garde," have passed into art or literary history as the most significant artists of their time. And, the combination of verbal and visual art is by no means a uniquely twentieth-century or "avant-garde" practice. The combination of the verbal and the visual has an astonishingly long lineage, and it is a mistake to consider the phenomenon as a whole as belonging to the avant-garde, although it is popularly considered to be anti-traditional.

The further we go back in time, the more frequently visual and verbal art forms were combined. In Egyptian art hieroglyphs were constantly combined with visual works of art, often integrated into many parts of the picture. A striking example, one chosen from many, is the wooden panels of Hesire carved during the Third Dynasty, where the hieroglyphs that explain the scenes depicted occur throughout the composition. The hieroglyphs are themselves pictorial, and they perhaps lent themselves better to visual integration than other alphabets. They presented special problems, as sometimes hieroglyphs can be read both as represented objects—parts of a realistic setting—and as accompanying text; in some works either a vertical or horizontal line or a change in the relief surface separated the hieroglyphs from the depicted scene.

The Greek and Roman alphabets were further removed from a pictorial basis. In early oral literature, quantitative form was based on the length and pitch of the vowel within the syllable; one of its functions was to serve as an aid to memory. Greek and Latin quantitative verse had little relation to visual art, especially in their early development. The verbal form stressed phonetic quantity, rhythm, and "choral" music rather than pictorial space. In early Chinese and Japanese art, however, the verbal text was frequently combined with a painting, especially on a scroll. This practice dates far back in oriental art history; once again, the verbal sign or character had a semi-pictorial nature that facilitated this integration, as well as the common medium of the brush that composed both words and picture.[1] The hand-painted characters easily adapted to the space of the painting and also to the shapes, for example, bamboo leaves or greenery. Frequently a lengthy narrative accompanied a painting or scroll, and the scroll or series of several scrolls recounted a story or historical episode.

Calligraphy was a highly developed form in the Far East and also in the Near East. It was a major art form in the Arab world where it was developed to an extreme degree of sophistication. The prohibition on naturalistic representation made it highly specialized, resulting in the form of the "arabesque" and the colorful ceramic or tile calligraphy that can

---

1. Ernest Fenollosa, "The Chinese Written Character as a Medium for Poetry," ed. Ezra Pound, in *The Little Review* (Chicago, 1919), repr. in Pound, *Instigations* (New York: Boni and Liveright, 1920).

be seen in the Alhambra (built between 1248 and 1354). Most of the verbal texts are taken from the Koran. A less specialized blend of verbal and visual elements can be seen in Near Eastern art; for example, in Persian painting the form of the words often blends with the floral forms, even with the belts, or sashes, of the costumes.

Calligraphy also became a highly developed art form in Europe during the Middle Ages. Manuscripts were copied by hand, and those which received the most lavish treatment were usually ecclesiastical: gospels, breviaries, pontificals, apocalypses, and codexes. Sometimes verbal and visual elements were only partly integrated, with the capital or initial letter introducing a sentence receiving the greatest pictorial elaboration, but in many of the finest manuscripts there is a remarkable degree of integration. The artist had little freedom for the manipulation of the verbal text—the word—that was sacred and of paramount importance. But the visual element was not necessarily rigidly enclosed by this text; on the contrary the visual rendering often profited from its participation with the sacred text and received a highly developed treatment, the subordination to the verbal text ensuring its integration with the verbal elements. An early example is the manuscript of the Lindisfarne Gospels, dating from before 721 A.D. Other later examples are the Book of Kells and the Belleville Breviary from the first half of the fourteenth century, where the illustrator has come into prominence and we know his name (Jean Pucelle).

Space is frequently given a three-dimensional treatment in these manuscripts, and perspective is present. The theological view of the world seemed to facilitate the passage from the essentially two-dimensional verbal text and manuscript surface to the three-dimensional space around it.

The Renaissance was a period of great proliferation of verse forms, most of them originally Italian or French and stressing the use of rhyme patterns. As with Greek and Latin quantitative verse, sound was again a major organizing element, with regular sound repetitions determining the formal rules of each particular type of poem: rondeau or rondeau redoublé, villanelle, sestina, ottava rima, ballade, triolet, chant royal, and many others. Unlike quantitative verse the graphic space on the page had great importance—stanza shape and indentation gave visual form to the poem; and rhyme, by occuring only at line endings, was both visual and auditory, welding the two into a strictly integrated pattern. Often contrast of line length was used for both auditory and visual effect—for example, in the nine-line stanza used by John Donne in his poem "A Valediction: Of Weeping," written in 1598:

> On a round ball
> A workman that hath copies by can lay
> An Europe, Afrique, and an Asia,
> And quickly make that, which was nothing, *All*.
> So doth each tear,
> Which thee doth wear,
> A globe, yea world by that impression grow,
> Till thy tears mixed with mine do overflow
> This world, by waters sent from thee, my heaven dissolved so.

Although the form is visual and graphic it is not, however, pictorial, and for the next three hundred years the pictorial aspect of poetry was to be in eclipse. The reasons are not far to seek: the emergence of printing in the sixteenth century coincided with the decline of calligraphy and manuscript illustration. The use of graphic form in poetry was adapted to the capacities of the printing press, and the original handwritten manuscript was relegated to the domain of the bibliographical scholar. The period of the next three hundred years corresponds to the growth of technology and industrialism. By a curious coincidence it also exactly corresponds to the growing concept of an extended "childhood," separate from adulthood and described earlier.

The change in attitude toward childhood was above all due to social need. From 1500 onwards the Western world grew ever more complex, demanding more skilled and trained men for commerce and the professions. This was also the time of the great empires—the French, the British, the Spanish, and the Dutch. Science and technology invaded more and more of economic and social life. From 1880 onwards their proliferation increased until they dominated the activities of Western society. Their growth demanded a longer and longer education, and this coincided with the separation of the world of childhood from that of adulthood, reaching a culmination in the nineteenth century when, in European upper classes, children were often excluded from adult society even in the home. In the arts this three-hundred-year period coincided with the dominance of perspective and a relative lack of integration of visual with verbal art forms. The period of the separation of the verbal and the visual coincides with the separation of the world of the child from that of the adult— although of course both visual fine arts and literature were genres practiced professionally by adults. Concepts of adulthood and expression in the arts had undergone related changes; it was just before the First World War, with the decline of the great empires and the psychoanalytic attack on Victorian concepts of a separate, innocent childhood, that attitudes began to change.

The French poet Guillaume Apollinaire developed the form of visual poems more than any other single poet. His point of departure was the typographical experimentation by Mallarmé in the long poem "Un coup de dés," but Apollinaire was even more radical than Mallarmé. It has been said one advantage of the picture poem is that it permits an entry into the poem that is simultaneous and total—it is not linear, with a top or bottom, left or right, but total, with the skeleton of the poem standing out visibly from the lesser members, the fundamental shape of the poem immediately detected. Apollinaire explained his use of the *calligramme* in the following manner:

As for the *Calligrammes,* they are an idealization of free-verse poetry and typographical preciseness at a time when typography is brilliantly terminating its career, at the dawn of new methods of reproduction, the cinema and the phonograph.[2]

It was rash to predict the end of the epoch of typography, which of course has not occurred. By his very invention of the *calligramme* he opened a new stage *within* the genre of typographical arrangement that was to become the concrete poem.

2. Roger Shattuck, ed., *The Selected Writings of Guillaume Apollinaire* (New York: New Directions, 1948).

The following poem entitled "Il pleut" (It's raining) presents rain falling in vertical columns made of words. It should be noted that effects of sound are not at all foreign to the picture poem; the first part of the poem is about the sound of rain and its evocations. A literal English translation of the poem would read:

it's raining women's voices as if they had died even in memory
and it's raining you as well marvellous encounters of my life
    O little drops
those rearing clouds begin to neigh a whole universe of auricular cities
listen if it rains while regret and disdain weep to an ancient music
listen to the bonds fall which hold you above and below

Much of the history of art and literature is the history of the alternation between contraction on the one hand and expansion on the other hand. Poetry has frequently felt the attraction of the visual arts—sometimes its pull is weaker and sometimes stronger. In the twentieth century, poets have tried to expand the expressive use of the margins on either side of the poem, and at times poetry has attempted to achieve a solidity similar to that of sculpture; this can be seen in the objects produced during the object-making period of the Surrealists in the 1930s, as well as in the "plastic poems" recently written (or rather, constructed). But painters often feel the equally strong attraction of verbal elements; four of the greatest painters in this century—Picasso, Braque, Miró, and Malevich—frequently incorporated words into their paintings. Witness also the term "literary" so often applied to paintings by art critics, and the importance of the titles of paintings—there is a constant temptation for the painter to make use of the words which surround him in everyday life, and which he must see wherever he looks. The desire to combine the verbal with the visual is nothing less than the desire to seek unity; it also represents the attempt to relate art forms to the reality in which we live, in all its breadth, meaning, and immediacy.

Analytical Cubism, developed by Picasso and Braque between 1909 and 1912, "analyzed" space into its various geometric planes that overlapped or ran into one another; it was revolutionary in its disregard of natural appearances. In 1912–13 paper-pasting or *collage* was introduced. This destroyed for the first time in hundreds of years the traditional technical integrity of the medium, which had been sacrosanct ever since the Gothic artists gave up adding gilded plaster halos to painted saints. *Collage* made use above all of what was close at hand; paintings by Picasso and Braque used parts of a newspaper, fragments of a song with words, or wallpaper. Through *collage* the Cubists not only broke the traditional integrity of the medium, but they also undermined what might be called the academic dignity of painting. "Look," said Picasso and Braque arrogantly, "we can make works of art out of the contents of waste baskets."[3]

Both Cubism and Futurism spread throughout Europe during the period just preceding and following World War I. Cubism also became very popular in prerevolutionary Russia. Just as Braque worked together with Picasso in the development of Cubism, at a greater distance the Russian painter Malevich followed their work from Moscow and painted his own Cubist works that were quite original, in some respects occasionally surpassing paintings by the

3. Alfred H. Barr, Jr., *Picasso: Fifty Years of His Art* (New York: Museum of Modern Art, 1946), p. 80.

IL PLEUT

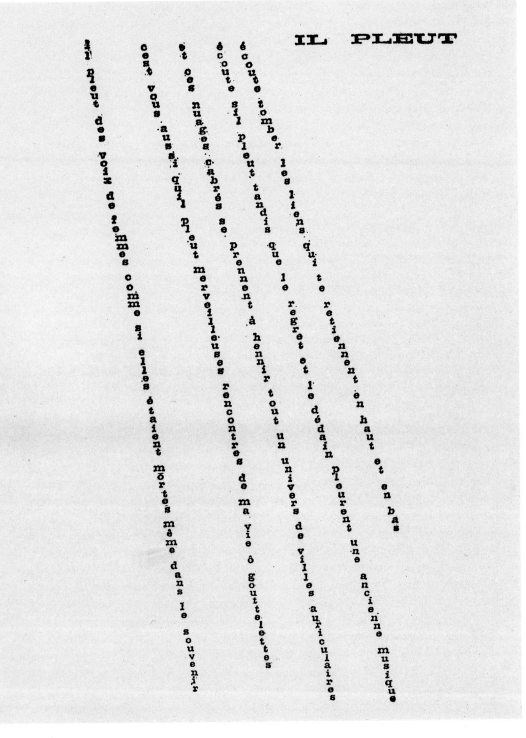

il pleut des voix de femmes comme si elles étaient mortes même dans le souvenir

c'est vous aussi qu'il pleut merveilleuses rencontres de ma vie ô gouttelettes

et ces nuages cabrés se prennent à hennir tout un univers de villes auriculaires

écoute s'il pleut tandis que le regret et le dédain pleurent une ancienne musique

écoute tomber les liens qui te retiennent en haut et en bas

French Cubists. In his painting "An Englishman in Moscow," enormous letters making scraps of words are accompanied by a series of objects: a tiny Russian church biting into an enormous fish, which in turn half obscures the top-hatted figure of an Englishman, a motto hanging like an epaulette at his shoulder with the Russian words for "Riding Club." A lit candle in a bedroom candlestick is suspended in midair, a ladder tips perilously, and a saber embraces the candle, ladder, and fish, everything suspended as if in a moment of experience, as if the man's thoughts were being described in a psychological study or a pictorial stream of consciousness.

At the same time that Cubism was spreading in Europe, the Italian poet F. T. Marinetti began the movement of Futurism in 1909 by publishing a manifesto in Paris, in *Le Figaro*. In 1913 he developed the concept of "words-in-freedom"; words were to be liberated above all from punctuation and syntax:

Suppose a friend of yours finds himself in a zone of intense life . . . what will he do? He will begin by brutally destroying the syntax of his speech. He wastes no time in building sentences. Punctuation and the right adjectives will mean nothing to him. He will despise subtleties and nuances of language. Breathlessly he will assault your nerves with visual, auditory, olfactory sensations, just as they come to him. The rush of steam-emotion will burst the sentence's steampipe, the valves of punctuation, and the adjectival clamp. Fistfulls of essential words in no conventional order. Sole preoccupation of the narrator, to render every vibration of his being.

He will cast immense nets of analogy across the world. In this way he will reveal the analogical foundation of life, telegraphically, with the same economical speed that the telegraph imposes on reporters and war correspondents in their swift reportings. . . . The poet's imagination must weave together distant things *with no connecting strings*, by means of essential *free* words.[4]

In works by the Cubists words were above all allied with everyday reality—with labels and names, titles, daily newspapers, what might be called the iconography of the city. It was the printed word that was usually imitated or reproduced, often in capitals as befits a title. The Surrealists approached words quite differently. Words were related to inner reality rather than outer, consequently the Surrealists stressed the handwritten (or painted) calligraphic line rather than the printed or capital letter. The Surrealist phase began in 1924 with an illusionist picture poem invented by Max Ernst, which was a three-dimensional projection of Apollinaire's *calligrammes*. The following year Joan Miró painted several of the finest picture poems ever made; they reflect the vogue of what the Surrealists called "automatism," or automatic writing that expressed the subconscious. The text of another picture poem by Miró, "A bird pursues a bee and ravishes it" ("Un oiseau / poursuit / une abeille / et la baisse"), describes the track of the pursuing bird, composed of a *collage* of feathers, and traced by the unwinding letters of the word "poursuit."

The more fluid, cursive, handwritten line preferred by Miró did not always follow straight horizontal lines. It was subtle and capricious, it could change direction, loop, rise, or descend depending on the meaning of the words and the visual shapes integrated with the words, as well as their colors. Miró's words are not abruptly cast or juxtaposed against a spatial background like the Cubists' labels, instead they flow into the background and penetrate it to a greater degree.

4. *Futurist Manifestos*, ed. Umbro Apollonio (New York: Viking, 1973) p. 98.

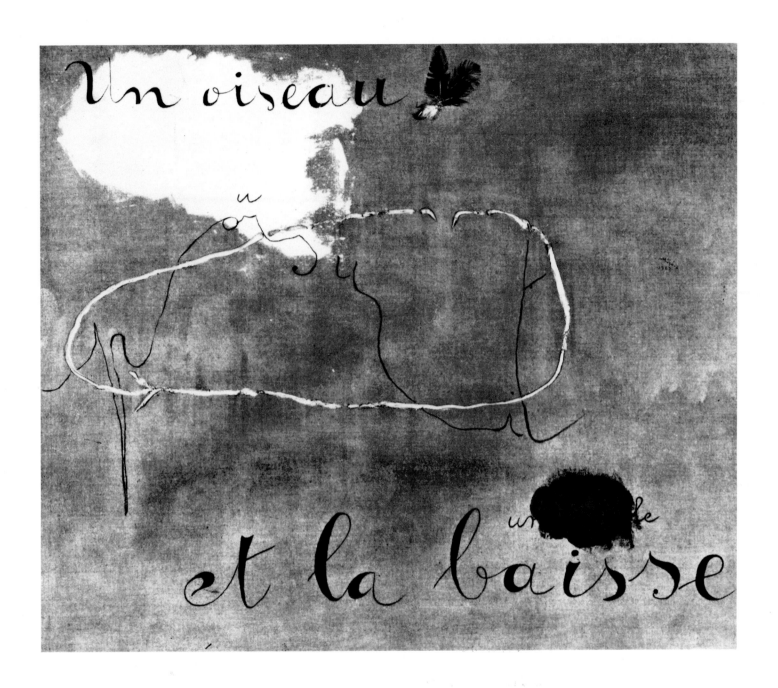

In literature and art the description of the outside objective world sometimes assumes greater importance, sometimes less. The Cubists perceived reality in a tactile manner, and in Braque's words they wanted "to take full possession of things." At almost the same time the Anglo-American Imagist movement, which began before World War I and continued after it, stressed imagery that was dependent on the use of the senses and emphasized the physical palpability of the world. Many of the ideas of the movement originated with the British aesthetician T. E. Hulme, who exerted a strong influence on the young Ezra Pound and less directly on T. S. Eliot. The American Objectivists had an abiding interest in the concrete world: William Carlos Williams wrote that there are "no ideas but in things" (in the poem, "A Sort of Song"). The Objectivists reacted against abstractions, symbols, and any modes of thought that were not "hard" or demonstrable.

Continental poets such as Rilke and Ponge stressed objects and "things" in their poetry, and one of the most talented poets of the period who worked within the Constructivist tradition, Julian Przyboś, saw the principal evolution of modern sensibility in the shifting of the creative effort from the subject to the object. In 1924 the French Surrealist André Breton had already proposed the fabrication of objects that appeared in dreams: he hoped to give concrete existence to these objects despite their strangeness and to bring into physical existence "veritable solidified desires." In 1936 he wrote in his essay, "The Crisis of the Object," that contemporary art was characterized by a "will toward objectivization without precedent." Breton was not interested in objective reality for its own sake, but rather in taking subjective reality and giving it objective expression. It was the pursuit of experience and the subconcious that he thought was important. Breton, influenced by Freud, proposed a number of different devices for expressing the subconcious. One of the most interesting was the poem-object, a miniature relief-assemblage in which various found objects were pasted to a picture surface and juxtaposed against fragments of poetry. In Breton's poems there was a very fluid passage from words to objects, facilitated by the lack of punctuation. The relation between them became increasingly tenuous until the object was almost completely emancipated from its verbal context.

Breton took the next step when he discarded words altogether and created what are known as "Surrealist objects." These were small non-sculptural constructions, a type of three-dimensional *collage* composed of found articles. They were attractive because they allowed the maker to escape all constraints of traditional artistic expression such as painting and sculpture and also of written poetry. They contained no words: they grew out of poetic experience and can best be judged as a "concrete" form of the Surrealist poetic image. The creation of these objects dominated the activities of the Surrealist circle until the outbreak of the Second World War. The relation between the verbal and the visual had been completely severed.

Not all periods are conducive to a balance of the verbal and the visual or between the individual and the space surrounding him, just as not all ages—or developmental stages— are conducive to this balance. The decade of the 1930s saw a gradual decline in concern with concrete textures and what might be called Imagistic practice, giving way to social and political concerns. Corporate pressures, whether of country, political group, or ideology, increased and no poets and artists could ignore them. It has been said that World War II had already been largely fought on an ideological level in the thirties before the actual fighting broke out; this can be clearly seen in the poetry of the thirties and also in the break between verbal and visual expression.

Three well-known poets who have written in English have paid some attention to the visual side of their verse—they are Ezra Pound, e. e. cummings, and Dylan Thomas. Of the three Thomas was the most radical in his use of space, which he often used to emphasize not only sound patterns in his poems but also rhythm. In "Fern Hill," for example, the indentations and variations of line length reinforce the lilting rhythm of the poem:

Now as I was young and easy under the apple boughs
About the lilting house and happy as the grass was green,
    The night above the dingle starry,
      Time let me hail and climb
    Golden in the heydays of his eyes,
And honoured among wagons I was prince of the apple towns
And once below a time I lordly had the trees and leaves
      Trail with daisies and barley
Down the rivers of the windfall light.

Another stanzaic shape is found in "Vision and Prayer," where a diamond-shaped stanza is used for the visionary sections of the poem, an hourglass pattern for the prayer sections:

I turn the corner of prayer and burn
In a blessing of the sudden
Sun. In the name of the damned
I would turn back and run
To the hidden land
But the loud sun
Christens down
The Sky.
I
Am found.
O let him
Scald me and drown
Me in his world's wound.
His lightning answers my
Cry. My voice burns in his hand.
Now I am lost in the blinding
One. The sun roars at the prayer's end.

In the 1950s and 1960s there was a great revival of interest in concrete poetry. It was widespread and international, extending from Europe to South and North America, and to Japan. Frequently the poems assume the form of the object they are written about. In this sense they are poems of definition, the words describing the object (or subject matter) of the poem above all in terms of its physical shape. Contemporary concrete poems often make use of machine graphics, avoiding the handwritten line. One of the effects of the "Pop" movement of the early 1960s was to discredit the expressive handwritten line and to steer concrete poetry toward the use of machine typography. The visual artists in the movement had the advantage of greater familiarity with graphic tools, while the poets often applied these tools to words as if they were exotic gadgets. At its best the Pop movement in concrete poetry made use of humor, parody, and playfulness; at its worst it combined naiveté about the use of graphics and *collage* with naiveté about expressiveness in the combination of words and pictorial forms, and ignored earlier attempts that had been made to combine the two.

In the future development of visual poetry the role of machine graphics will probably be crucial. Poets frequently have no training in this field, which requires an acquaintance with a specific technology. Occasionally poets have entered into fruitful collaborations with artists. Curiously, attempts to preserve the handwritten cursive line are being made more frequently by visual artists than by poets, who opt more often for typography. Yet it is difficult to integrate typography and machine graphics with three-dimensional space. The machine, if not used as a tool subordinate to expression, can easily act as a barrier between the individual poet or artist and the space which surrounds him.

6 / Conclusion

This book has combined a study of two types of imagination used by children and by adults, the verbal and the visual. They might have been considered separately, but in that case there is a strong likelihood the conclusions would have been different. The great advantage in considering them together is that they reinforce a single conclusion: the separation of the verbal and the visual is not grounded in the structure of reality, nor in psychology—it is accidental rather than inevitable. The variety of combinations of the two is very great but the two will always be close together in our minds when we express our relation to the world. A large number of studies of the arts avoid this issue and ignore the fact that the artist deals with ordinary reality, with the world, trying to give it form or integrate it. Art and literature as individual genres with their own traditions, their history and their techniques—these are familiar. I have chosen, instead, to emphasize the individual's relation to the world and the creative act itself. The study of visual poetry by children shows that visual expression naturally accompanies verbal expression, although in different ways depending on the child's age, with different elements held in a balance that is always dynamic and liable to change. The adult use of spatial form in poetry has an extremely ancient lineage, and poetry has always distinguished itself from prose by its use of graphic space as well as varying degrees of visual stylization. As with the different stages of the child, different historical periods—both in the arts and in literature—have favored different devices for balancing the two and expressing a view of the world. Often called traditions, one of their dominant characteristics, however, is that they frequently change and occur in different combinations. What is constant is that the verbal and visual are so close together in one combination or another that they are never kept separate for long. The visual imagination is always active and simultaneous, to a greater or lesser degree, with the verbal imagination.

The normal horizontal printed line can make many visual effects both in prose and poetry without recourse to graphic form, or mimetic shapes that disturb the even flow of the lines from one margin to the other; words alone can create highly developed imagery. So it might be asked, Why then should there be a need for additional form, which at its worst might be distracting? Certainly no argument could demonstrate that picture poems or mixed media are in any way superior to the great works created in a single genre. On the contrary, works of a single genre are often superior. And yet poetry as a genre is mixed, as we have shown, and so is painting. The creative use of space on the page grows out of poetry's traditional use of graphic space, variable margins and stanzas; it is merely an extension of an old practice and completely traditional in its origins. Once the choice is made to use poetry as opposed to prose or another genre, the use of variable margins and space is already accepted; the only question remaining is how much graphic or visual form will be used—how expressive will be the line endings, the stanza divisions, to what extent will the verbal imagery be given pictorial form? If the author elects not to give graphic emphasis to his lines, this will at least be a conscious choice with an awareness of the alternatives.

One of the major aspirations of twentieth-century art and science, to which they have devoted a large part of their productive energy, is the exploration of the nature of reality. When we review the various artistic movements of the past eighty years, the theme of the exploration of the world is dominant. A number of theoreticians, both poets and critics, have thought that the major trend of twentieth-century poetry has been toward objectivization, whether by exploring tangible, particular reality with an Objectivist like W. C. Williams, or by descending into the domain of the subconscious with the Surrealists—one of them, André Breton, spent much of his effort in trying to find the concrete objects that corresponded to the inner life of the psyche. In both cases this has meant the integration of the individual with all his inner reality and psychological depth to the outer world of things, of concrete objects and space.

Clearly the synthesis of the visual with the verbal occupies a major role in twentieth-century literature and art, whether it is in the domain of the purely verbal image or whether the image is given more graphic, pictorial form. In every artistic genre (and this applies also to science) there is a tendency to try to give expression to what has not yet been given expression before. In this process of objectivization neither the word "objective" nor "subjective" accurately applies because it involves active participation with reality, experience in the case of art, the experiment in the case of science. Neither word alone applies to our relationship to reality, to space. In literature the synthesis can take place within each separate genre without necessarily crossing the frontier to another genre, but probably this will constantly, even inevitably, approach the limit of the genre and will naturally attempt to pass beyond it—for there are no "natural" limits to the genres of either poetry or painting, as we have tried to show.

Although the exploration of the world has been one of the dominant themes of twentieth-century art and literature, this fact is not always noticed for what it is. Literary studies often focus on purely literary relationships and questions of influence, ignoring the exploratory function of literature or art and its relation to the world. The separation of genres creates specialization and a certain self-conciousness in each one that tends to sever its relationship with other genres and aspects of life; this in turn creates new "genres" such as the self-conscious novel or poem.[1] The verbal and visual are inextricably bound together, and it is only in subsequent artistic treatment, in the privacy of the studio or study, that the two artistic modes are usually separated, or at a still later stage in a library classification, curriculum, or academic department. Many authors of specialized artistic and literary studies find it convenient to focus almost exclusively on questions of influence and to ignore the exploratory function of art, as well as the closeness of the visual and verbal imagination. An extreme example is a recent book interpreting the major writers of the nineteenth and twentieth centuries by their "oedipal" reactions to a dominant, famous writer of the older generation who influenced them as a "surrogate father."[2]

1. Robert Alter, *Partial Magic: The Novel as a Self-Conscious Genre* (Berkeley: University of California Press, 1975).
2. Harold Bloom, *The Anxiety of Influence* (New York: Oxford University Press, 1973).

At the inception of the creative act no immediate separation takes place into a verbal or visual genre; it is later that limitations of genre are emphasized rather than minimized—self-consciousness of treatment and the type of stylization that is dis-integrative rather than integrative may occur. In dealing with artistic products, we find our attention easily shifts to the product considered as object. The "limitations" of a genre originally based on considerations of mechanical reproduction, distribution, or library storage come to be no longer purely technical matters but influence the conception of the creative act itself, our expectation of what it can or should be. What was originally a technological process at the service of the creative act becomes a product limiting and even defining the nature of the creative act itself.

The reasons for stressing artistic or literary relationships are obvious: "the world" and "reality" are difficult concepts to define or manipulate. They are easily accused of imprecision, for they border on a variety of more or less unfamiliar fields and are not amenable to a technical or specialized vocabulary. In this book I have tried to be as precise as possible when speaking about "the world" and especially one aspect of it, the relation of the verbal and the visual imagination, in an effort to redress the balance. To do this I have referred to two and sometimes more art forms. In exploring the relation between the individual and the world in these art forms, I have also referred to writers of very different ages—this has permitted us to study the closeness between the visual and the verbal in a large variety of combinations, and to form an idea of the almost infinite number of possibilities for integrating them.

There are many signs of impatience with existing forms on the part of both younger and older poets. In the 1960s and 1970s there was much experimentation with partial or total elimination of punctuation, or the use of spaces in the middle of the poetic line. The expressive use of sound in poetry is also being explored. In the visual arts there is much experimentation with verbal forms. Some of the revolt is tentative: young artists are often eager to revolt against their predecessors, but find it difficult to conceive of the world in a manner different from these predecessors. The result is often a quarrel of choice of influence while the basic attitude toward reality remains accepted or virtually untouched. However, twentieth-century art has come to have a major function that is not self-conscious, and could be called a tradition if it were not based on the dynamic relation between the individual and the world around him: that of exploration. It is radical and has come to be a constant. Experiment becomes very rapidly accepted and absorbed. This is reinforced by the questioning of traditions resulting from World War II and what has come to be known as the Holocaust; in many European countries, especially those that were occupied or destroyed, the use of art, of language, and the very nature of reality have been thrown open to doubt.

There will always be a practical need to reproduce texts and pictures, to distribute, promote, and store works of art. How this need is met will depend partly on the technology available, and the processes will naturally stress simplification, clarification, and reduction in order to communicate. On the other hand, there will always be the counter-tendency to condense and to integrate in the serious arts. The entire world of experience and of space—both the outer world of reality and the inner world of the psyche, equally real—awaits the artist and every individual, manifold, rich, available, and inexhaustible.

Bibliography

Some helpful books on children's writing and their developmental stages are:

Aries, Philippe. *Centuries of Childhood.* New York: Alfred A. Knopf, 1962.

Arnstein, Flora. *Children Write Poetry.* New York: Dover, 1967.

_____. *Poetry in the Elementary Classroom.* New York: Appleton Century Croft, 1962.

Bettelheim, Bruno. *The Uses of Enchantment.* New York: Random House, 1976.

_____. *The Empty Fortress.* New York: Macmillan, 1967.

Erikson, Erik. *Childhood and Society.* New York: W. W. Norton, 1950.

Formanek, Ruth, and Gurian Formanek. *Charting Intellectual Development.* Springfield, Ill.: Thomas Pub., 1976.

Getzels, Jacob W., and Philip Jackson. *Creativity and Intelligence.* New York: Wiley, 1962.

Ginsburg, Herbert, and Sylvia Opper. *Piaget's Theory of Intellectual Development.* Englewood Cliffs, N.J.: Prentice-Hall, 1979.

Huizinga, Johan. *Homo Ludens.* New York: Harper and Row, 1970.

Kellogg, Rhoda. *Analyzing Children's Art.* Palo Alto, Calif.: National Press Books, 1969.

_____. *The Psychology of Children's Art.* San Diego, Calif.: Random House, 1967.

Koch, Kenneth. *Wishes, Lies, and Dreams.* New York: Random House, 1973.

Kosinski, Leonard V., ed. *Readings on Creativity and Imagination in Literature and Language.* Champaign, Ill.: National Council of Teachers of English, 1968.

Kubie, Lawrence S. *Neurotic Distortion of the Creative Process.* Lawrence, Kan.: University of Kansas Press, 1958.

Lopate, Phillip. *Being with Children.* Garden City, N.Y.: Doubleday, 1975.

Piaget, Jean. *Biology and Knowledge.* Chicago: University of Chicago Press, 1971.

_____. *The Child's Perception of Space.* New York: W. W. Norton, 1967.

_____. *The Grasp of Consciousness.* Cambridge: Harvard University Press, 1976.

_____. *The Mechanics of Perception.* New York: Basic Books, 1969.

Schachtel, Ernest G. *Metamorphosis: On the Development of Affect, Perception, Attention, and Memory.* New York: Basic Books, 1959.

Scribner, Sylvia, and Michael Cole. *The Psychology of Literacy.* Cambridge: Harvard University Press, 1980.

Spacks, Patricia Meyer. *The Adolescent Idea.* New York: Basic Books, 1980.

Winnicott, D. W. *Playing and Reality.* London: Tavistock, 1971.

_____. *Through Pediatrics to Psychoanalysis.* New York: Basic Books, 1974.

The following books are useful collections of visual poetry or art with verbal elements:

Apollinaire, Guillaume. *Calligrammes.* Paris: Gallimard, 1925.

_____. *Selected Writings of Guillaume Apollinaire.* Translated and edited by Roger Shattuck. New York: New Directions, 1958.

Apollonio, Umbro, ed. *Futurist Manifestoes.* New York: Viking, 1973.

Between Poetry and Painting. Catalogue of the Institute of Contemporary Arts. London, 1965.

Bowlt, John, ed. *Modern Russian Masters.* New York: Viking, 1977.

Fry, Edward F. *Cubism.* London: Thames on Hudson, 1966.

Geiger 1968—Experimental Anthology. Torino, Italy, 1968.

Habasque, Guy. *Cubism.* Cleveland: Skira-World, 1959.

Hollander, John. *Types of Shape.* New York: Atheneum, 1967.

Kostelanetz, Richard, ed. *Visual Literature Criticism.* Carbondale: Southern Illinois University Press, 1980.

_____. *Imaged Words and Worded Images.* New York: Outerbridge and Dienstfrey, 1970.

_____. *Illuminations.* New York: Laughing Bear, 1977.

Rubin, William. *Dada, Surrealism, and Their Heritage.* New York: Museum of Modern Art, 1968.

Solt, Mary, ed. *Concrete Poetry: A World View.* Bloomington: University of Indiana Press, 1970.

Williams, Emmett, ed. *An Anthology of Concrete Poetry.* New York: Something Else Press, 1967.